D0312516

Becoming
MADELEINE

Madeleine, circa 1924

Becoming MADELEINE

A BIOGRAPHY OF THE AUTHOR OF
A WRINKLE IN TIME BY HER GRANDDAUGHTERS

Charlotte Jones Voiklis *and* Léna Roy

Farrar Straus Giroux
New York

Farrar Straus Giroux Books for Young Readers
An imprint of Macmillan Publishing Group, LLC
175 Fifth Avenue, New York, NY 10010

Printed in the United States of America by LSC Communications, Harrisonburg, Virginia
Designed by Roberta Pressel
First edition, 2018

1 3 5 7 9 10 8 6 4 2

mackids.com

The images and photographs in this book come from the authors' family collection,
used with the permission of Crosswicks, Ltd., with the exception of the following:
Page 39: Courtesy of Collection Musée de Montreux, Switzerland; Page 43: Courtesy of Ashley Hall;
Page 49: Courtesy of Ashley Hall; Page 64: Courtesy of Ashley Hall; Page 83: Courtesy of the New York
Public Library Digital Collections; Page 152: Courtesy of Farrar Straus Giroux Books for Young
Readers; Page 153: Courtesy of Farrar Straus Giroux Books for Young Readers

Library of Congress Cataloging-in-Publication Data

Names: Voiklis, Charlotte Jones author. | Roy, Léna author.
Title: Becoming Madeleine : a biography of the author of A Wrinkle in Time
   by her granddaughters / Charlotte Jones Voiklis and Léna Roy.
Description: First edition. | New York : Farrar Straus Giroux, 2018.
Identifiers: LCCN 2017014004 (print) | LCCN 2017027369 (ebook) |
   ISBN 9780374307653 (ebook) | ISBN 9780374307646 (hardcover)
Subjects: LCSH: L'Engle, Madeleine—Juvenile literature. | Authors,
   American—20th century—Biography—Juvenile literature.
Classification: LCC PS3523.E55 (ebook) | LCC PS3523.E55 Z885 2017 (print) |
   DDC 813/.54 [B]—dc23
LC record available at https://lccn.loc.gov/2017014004

Our books may be purchased in bulk for promotional, educational, or business use.
Please contact your local bookseller or the Macmillan Corporate and Premium Sales Department
at (800) 221-7945 ext. 5442 or by e-mail at MacmillanSpecialMarkets@macmillan.com.

For Greatie, Dannie, Dearma, Grachie,
GrandMadeleine, Jamma,
and all grandmothers

Contents

A self is not something static, tied up in a pretty parcel
and handed to the child, finished and complete.
A self is always becoming.
—Madeleine L'Engle, *A Circle of Quiet*

Becoming MADELEINE

Charlotte, Madeleine, and Léna, circa 1973

Prologue

We were young when our grandmother, Madeleine L'Engle, started sharing with us the patchwork of events, relationships, and emotions that shaped her into the person she was always becoming. She described her childhood as solitary, and we thought it must have been lonely—after all, even we, who had each other, had periods of loneliness. But her stories about growing up and becoming the writer and grandmother we knew gave us the assurance that, just like her, we could survive the hurts and joys of childhood and adolescence.

She encouraged us to read whatever we wanted, and eventually what we wanted was to read her books. By the time we were nine and ten, we had read *A Wrinkle in Time*, *A Wind in the Door*, and various excerpts of *A Swiftly Tilting Planet*, which was about to be published. The stories *felt* like Gran because they were infused with her spirit and took place at her home in Connecticut. However, it wasn't until we read *And Both Were Young*, a novel she had written about a girl at a Swiss boarding school, that we recognized a direct parallel to her life. We knew that she had also gone to a boarding school in Switzerland, and we wondered if everything that happened to Flip, the protagonist, had happened to her, too. So we asked.

"Were the other girls mean to you?"

"Did you plant poppies hoping for wonderful dreams?"

"Were you really called by a number and not your name?"

She patiently answered our questions and went on to tell us how she came to go to the school in the first place. She was only eleven, shy, awkward, and bookish. She and her parents had moved to rural France, and on a beautiful day in late September they had packed a picnic lunch and started driving. Madeleine had assumed they were going to spend the afternoon on the shores of Lake Geneva, in Switzerland, but instead they passed a sign for the village of Montreux and pulled up to Châtelard, a boarding school for girls. It was grand on the outside, cold and spare on the inside. Her parents introduced her to the school's matron and left her there, with hardly a word of goodbye.

"Really, Gran?" Our regal but sensitive grandmother abandoned at a foreign boarding school, her parents too cowardly to tell her what they were doing? We were outraged.

"It wasn't so bad after a while," she assured us. "And I learned a lot. It helped me become a writer." She then went on to explain, "I had always written stories, ever since I could hold a pencil. As a small child in New York City, I spent a good deal of time alone, and my stories kept me company. But at boarding school, I was never alone. They didn't think that privacy was good for girls. So I learned to shut out the din of a crowded dormitory, and now I can concentrate and write anywhere."

We were still incredulous. "But weren't you angry with your parents? How did you ever forgive them?"

"Of course I was angry. And hurt, too. But I came to

realize my parents had their own hurts and angers that had nothing to do with me. Before the war, before I was born, they lived a very adventurous and happy life. But then after the war came along and I was born, everything changed for them. Trying to make sense of all of this helped me become a writer. A writer must be able to understand different points of view."

Still, the story was grim. After the first couple of months at Châtelard, Madeleine was able to go home for Christmas vacation, but instead of a joyous reunion, with parents delighted to see their only child, she found her parents withdrawn and unhappy. Her father was ill and his typewriter sat unused. Her mother played Bach on the piano with fury. They were too wrapped up in their own worries and sadness to give her much attention.

"How did you get over that?"

"I tried to understand them. I wrote stories, trying to imagine what it was like for them. I learned to inhabit other selves, other ages. It helped put things into perspective. And now that I am older, I still do that. I've never had to lose my younger selves—so that's why I am every age I have ever been."

We've been wondering and marveling at her timelessness ever since.

We are now able to step back and look at how our grandmother became Madeleine L'Engle, starting from the beginning: What were her parents like when they had been happy, before World War I, before she was born? How did her hurts and joys manifest themselves in her writing? Here, with the aid of her fiction and nonfiction books—along with her journals, letters, and our own family stories and memories—we begin to answer the questions.

Charles Wadsworth Camp and Madeleine "Mado" Hall Barnett, circa 1908

Before Madeleine

Madeleine's mother, Madeleine "Mado" Hall Barnett, grew up in Jacksonville, a city in northern Florida on the Atlantic Ocean. She was a classically trained concert pianist who had studied in Berlin.

Madeleine's father, Charles Wadsworth Camp, was a novelist and journalist. He was born near and educated at Princeton University, "up North" in New Jersey.

In many ways they were opposites. Charles at twenty-eight was gregarious, confident, and handsome—over six feet tall, with thick fair hair. Mado was much more reserved. She had always felt herself to be an ugly duckling, and at twenty-six she was considered an old maid.

They met when Charles came to Jacksonville for his sister's wedding. Mado was standoffish at first, unsure that his attentions were sincere. But they quickly fell in love and married in 1906, and Charles whisked her off to New York City.

Mado and Charles settled in a two-bedroom apartment on East Eighty-Second Street. Charles reviewed plays, wrote novels, and later was a foreign correspondent for magazines such as *Collier's* and *The Century*. He traveled abroad frequently for his work, taking steamships across the ocean to

Mado, circa 1904

places like London and Paris as well as Cairo and Shanghai, and was often accompanied by Mado. Charles's work also meant that he and Mado rubbed elbows with both high society and a world of artists. Although they loved to entertain, they couldn't afford to throw lavish dinner parties, so they instituted a tradition of simple Sunday-night suppers. Their friends would pile into their tiny apartment, a few of them would cook a meal, and Mado would play the piano while they all sang. Everyone had a glorious time. (Mado enjoyed playing for friends and at small gatherings, but she was terrified about playing in public.)

Then came the outbreak of World War I in 1914. Charles went to Europe twice for magazines—first to cover the war in France in 1914, and then to report on the Easter Rising in Ireland in 1916. He also wrote a nonfiction book about that experience called *War's Dark Frame*, published in 1917, just before the United States entered the war.

Charles enlisted in the army as a second lieutenant and was sent to fight in France in 1918.

His war experience, as both a journalist and a soldier, had a deep impact on him that reverberated throughout his and his family's life. When describing her father, Madeleine recalled that he was horrified and repelled by the destruction and devastation he had witnessed. Later, Madeleine said

Charles, circa 1900

Charles, 1917

that the war had killed him; it just took him seventeen years to die. She, too, had a lifelong terror of war.

Mado and Charles both desperately wanted children, and had been trying for more than ten years. Charles, the youngest child and only boy in his family of six girls, was eager to have a boy to carry on the family name. When Charles was deployed in early 1918, Mado was two months pregnant.

Even though Armistice was declared later that year, on November 11, Charles was still on active duty when, early in the morning on November 29, the day after Thanksgiving, Mado went into labor.

It must have been a difficult delivery, because Mado wasn't able to write to Charles until two weeks later.

December 13, 1918
My dearest husband—

If you could see your little flower of a daughter, I am sure you would forgive her for not being a boy. Oh my dear, I am so thankful that she is here and healthy and perfect and I wouldn't exchange her now for all the sons in the world.

She is considered a perfect miracle in the hospital and every one is interested in us, and so if you were only here to share my happiness. It is worth all the long months of waiting and the hours of agony at the end. Dear one, I have been pretty sick and am hoisted up in bed for the first time this afternoon. Baby is two weeks old today. [A cousin] phoned yesterday that your mother had sent you a cable yesterday afternoon. I wonder if you have had mine sent November 30 and if you know what a proud father you should be? It seems so strange not to have heard from you yet. I got your letter of Nov 21 a day or two ago. There was nothing between that and the one of Nov 13 I received Thanksgiving Day, so I must have lost one at least.

I do hope you have had a nice time on your leave and that your cold is gone. I have worried over your ears, dear. Never mind about the promotion dear. It is hard luck but lots of others have been treated the same way and I am so happy that you are safe and whole. Nothing else matters. Have you any idea yet when you are coming home? It can't be so long, yet every week will seem an eternity now.

I have two good nurses dear. My day nurse is the very best in the whole world I am sure. I just love her dearly and she is good to me and the baby. I hope you approve of baby's name—Madeleine L'Engle. I think it just suits her and thought you would want her named Madeleine. I must stop now dear. I'm pretty wobbly but very very happy.

Will try to write again in a day or so.

Your loving wife, Madeleine

Mado with Madeleine, 1919

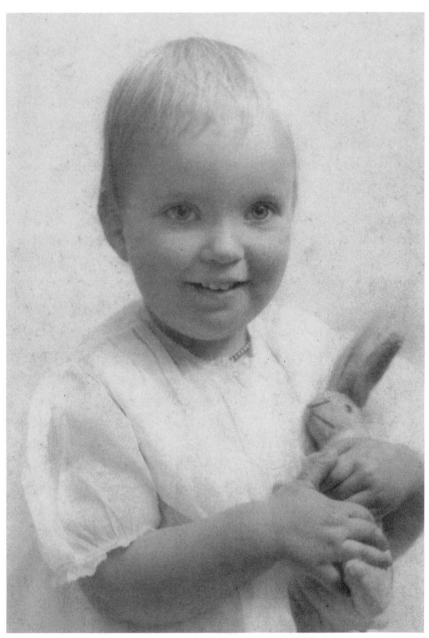

Madeleine, circa 1920

A New York City Childhood

When Charles finally returned to New York in May 1919, he and Mado were thrilled that the war was over, that they were back together, and that they had their much-longed-for child. Charles resumed his work as a journalist, reviewing plays and writing his own plays, novels, and short stories.

Madeleine's parents loved her, but the pattern of their married life had already been well established over the twelve years they had been together before she was born: dinner at eight, adult conversation, evenings out, and sleeping in. Even as a young child, Madeleine was content eating alone in her room—with her feet on her desk and her plate on her chest—and going to bed before her parents sat down to their more elegant grown-up dinners.

They often went to plays, operas, and symphonies, and they would come and kiss her good night before they left, her father in top hat and tails, smelling comfortingly of Egyptian tobacco, whiskey, and starched linen, and her mother also elegantly dressed and smelling deliciously of expensive perfume.

Her parents still had those casual Sunday-night suppers, and Madeleine would sometimes sneak out of bed and listen from the hallway to the music and the conversation. While

Charles and Madeleine, circa 1919

some children might have observed and fantasized about being a grown-up someday, Madeleine saw it as fascinating and curious, but not something she wanted for herself. She sensed that childhood was only very short in the scheme of things, and she wanted it to last.

Her parents, however, disagreed about how to raise her. Mado hadn't had much formal education, spending her childhood in Florida with lots of cousins and play. She thought childhood should be carefree. Charles had had a much more traditional school experience and therefore wanted a more structured upbringing for his daughter. Charles usually won their disagreements, and he was insistent about sending his daughter to the best schools, whether his daughter liked it or not, and whether he and his wife could afford it or not. (His pocketbook, Mado was fond of saying, "waxed and waned like the moon.")

Charles was prone to depression and sometimes withdrew from his wife and child. When he emerged from his darkness and turned his attention once more toward his daughter, it was as if the sun were shining on her again. His moodiness did not stop Madeleine from adoring her father, and being a little bit in awe of him. He was a force in the world: charismatic, confident, and charming. She watched him writing, absorbed in his creation of stories—real and fictional—and saw that it gave him both pleasure and frustration. He wrote a first draft in longhand and then typed it out on a typewriter. As a war correspondent, he typed his dispatches directly. When Madeleine was ten, he gave her his old typewriter, which she used into the 1950s.

Charles, Madeleine, and Mado, circa 1922

Charles's typewriter, given to Madeleine at age ten

One of the ways her father shared his love of stories with his daughter was through opera. The first time he took her was when she was around eight. It was a production of *Madame Butterfly*. Madeleine had no idea what to expect, but she was immediately drawn into the story and the music. It started like a beautiful fairy tale, a love story between a naval officer and a young Japanese woman. But when tragedy befell Cio-Cio-San at the end, Madeleine was deeply shocked and upset. She didn't want to disappoint her father, so when he asked if

she had enjoyed the opera, she said that she had, and he had no idea that she was traumatized by the sad ending. The next time he took her to see an opera—*Pagliacci*—she asked him as they sat down if this story had an unhappy ending, too. When he told her it did, she began to cry

Madeleine and Caroline "Dearma" Barnett, circa 1922

Mado and Madeleine, circa 1924

and did not stop until her father took her home, before the curtain even rose.

Madeleine spent more time with her mother, who was often home practicing the piano for hours at a time or writing daily letters to the family and friends she had left behind in Jacksonville. The two would visit Jacksonville several times a year, traveling on the overnight train. They stayed with Madeleine's grandmother Caroline Barnett, whom Madeleine called "Dearma." There were lots of cousins there, too.

Like Charles, Mado was a wonderful storyteller. Many of the stories she told Madeleine were about Mado's grandmother, the first Madeleine L'Engle, who had had not only a glamorous adolescence in Spain in the 1840s as the daughter of the U.S. ambassador, but also adventurous early days of marriage to an army doctor traveling throughout America's western territories and across the Isthmus of Panama before there was a canal. Then, widowed early during the Civil War, Mado's grandmother had worked as a nurse at an army hospital and eventually settled in Jacksonville.

Madeleine with unknown boys, circa 1923

Mado would also recount stories that her father, Bion Barnett, had told her about his wild childhood in Kansas. He would tell his children the stories after dinner, while he smoked a cigar, and Mado always kept an eye on his lengthening ash, knowing that when it fell, the stories were over for the evening.

Madeleine and her parents traveled by ship to Europe several times when she was young, visiting Grandfather Bion, that cigar-smoking storyteller, and his common-law wife, Louise, whom Madeleine and her cousins called "Gaga." Grandfather Bion was a wealthy banker who lived in various places in France and Monte Carlo. Later Madeleine would recall idyllic wanderings around the French countryside, provisioned with bitter chocolate, sweet butter, and sour bread, which she said taught her how to mix flavors and textures in both her cooking and her writing.

Aside from her parents, the adult who meant the most to her was Mrs. O'Connell. Mary O'Connell—whom Madeleine called Mrs. O—came several times a week to the Camps' New York apartment to help Mado with the cooking and cleaning, and she took a special shine to the young Madeleine. And Madeleine adored her. Next to her strict and formal parents, Mrs. O was a breath of freedom and a glimpse into a wider world. Mrs. O, who thought Madeleine was overprotected, would often bend the rules.

For example, Madeleine was confined to her Upper East Side neighborhood, but Mrs. O took her on the subway to other parts of the city—on adventures to Greenwich Village and even to the Bronx, where Mrs. O lived. A devout Roman Catholic, Mrs. O would sometimes take Madeleine to church to attend Mass or to light a candle for someone in pain or trouble. But Madeleine and Mrs. O agreed to keep these outings a secret because they knew her parents would not have approved.

Madeleine also loved exploring her Upper East Side neighborhood with her parents or Mrs. O—the tree-lined streets; the tall, elegant buildings; and especially the Metropolitan Museum of Art. She visited its galleries whenever she could, enthralled by the creativity and history on display. Her girlhood memories of New York City remained strong throughout her life, and she always thought of it as her home.

Madeleine, circa 1924

21

Madeleine, circa 1924

Trouble at School

Madeleine enjoyed school in the early grades, but things changed in the fourth grade, when she switched schools, and going to class started to become a painful, diminishing experience. With one leg slightly shorter than the other, she didn't have the same athletic prowess as her classmates and so was always picked last for any team. She quickly gained a reputation for being both clumsy and stupid, for she was shy and reticent. Her peers treated her badly, and her teachers graded her to their own expectations instead of Madeleine's actual performance. Thus Madeleine learned that making an effort for the teacher simply wasn't worth it. When she went home, instead of doing homework, she turned to her own reading and writing. Grandfather Bion sent her books and magazines, and she wrote stories. After all, that's what her father did. She also wrote poetry.

One day that first year at her new school, Madeleine's French teacher refused to let her go to the bathroom even though she asked repeatedly to be excused. And so she wet her pants. When questioned by Mado and the headmistress, the teacher defended herself by lying, saying that Madeleine had never asked to be excused. But Mado believed Madeleine, and that was a comfort, although watching an adult lie and get away with it was devastating to Madeleine.

The next year, in fifth grade, there was a poetry contest that was open to the entire school and judged blindly. Madeleine entered one of her poems. When it won and she was revealed as the writer, her teacher insisted that Madeleine couldn't possibly have written such a good poem and accused her of plagiarism. Outraged and indignant, Mado took samples of Madeleine's poetry to the school and showed them to both the headmistress and the teacher, who was forced to concede that Madeleine was a good enough writer to have written that poem after all.

Portraits

Prize Poem

I

Dᴵᴰ you ever come alive,
Portaits painted on the wall?
Don't you ever walk about,
And laugh and sing at all?

II

The museum is full of people,
But that doesn't matter, you see,
They don't know that the portraits
Are laughing and smiling at me.

III

There's a fisherman in his boat,
A lady all in white,
And knights and kings on horses,
So glittering and bright.

IV

There's a pretty little girl,
With golden hair so long,

It falls over her shoulders so softly
As she seems to be singing a song.

V

Oh, little girl with long stiff skirts,
Don't you ever walk about?
I think, little boy, who plays with her
You must sometimes laugh and shout.

VI

There's Washington crossing the
Delaware.
And Lincoln, lanky and long.
Ah, these heroes of our country
Were so brave and kind and strong.

VII

Portraits hanging on the wall,
Don't you ever walk about?
Don't you ever play and sing,
Don't you ever laugh and shout?
              Madeleine Camp, Class Five

65

Madeleine's prize poem, published in the school literary magazine, May 1929

24

Madeleine, circa 1926

When Madeleine wasn't reading and writing after school, she was taking art and piano lessons. She was also forced to take dance lessons, which she detested so much that her instructors proclaimed she was "unteachable." It was a pretty miserable—as well as formative—few years: from then on, Madeleine carried with her the feeling that she was awkward, inadequate, unattractive, and stupid, feelings that made her acutely grateful for any acts of kindness and affection that she did receive from others.

Madeleine did have one friend with whom she played occasionally. April Warburg, the daughter of a wealthy banker, was as much of an outcast at school as Madeleine was, and just as dreamy. Sometimes Madeleine would go over to April's house, a mansion on Fifth Avenue. April's parents weren't around, but there were multiple servants—butlers, ladies' maids, governesses—and Madeleine was struck by the different kind of isolation April endured: one in which she was not alone, but lonely. She saw how removed her friend was from her parents and from affection of any kind, and she was thankful for her own relatively close relationship with her mother and father.

Then Madeleine's father's health started to fail. When he was in the army, his unit had been gassed by enemy forces during the war, and the effects of the mustard gas had left him prone to severe and life-threatening bouts of pneumonia. He also smoked and drank heavily, which exacerbated his fits of coughing and his headaches. Mado was worried about Charles's health, but he seemed more concerned with the fact that his writing work was drying up—it was difficult to support a family as a freelance journalist, and his fiction wasn't selling as it had before the war. He caught pneumonia and was warned that he should find a more healthy place to live: the dirty, smoggy air of New York City might kill him. Could they possibly leave the city? Their life was there. If it was difficult getting writing assignments in New York, how much harder would it be elsewhere?

And then the stock market crashed in October 1929, and a great many people were in financial trouble, including Madeleine's parents. They decided they had no other choice:

the summer after Madeleine finished sixth grade, they packed their clothes; put their furniture, piano, dishes, and silver into storage; and moved to the French Alps, where there was clean mountain air and where, at that time, it would be less expensive to live.

Madeleine, circa 1931

Switzerland

Madeleine, unaware of her parents' perilous circumstances, was thrilled with the move. Fresh air! Freedom from school! Parents not distracted by social events! And there were more opportunities to see Grandfather Bion and Gaga as well as her uncle Bion (Mado's brother) and his children, her cousins. Uncle Bion was an artist who had married a Frenchwoman, and they lived in Corsica. The summer of 1930 was filled with whimsy for the eleven-year-old Madeleine: she roamed around on her own in the French countryside and read *Emily of New Moon* by Lucy Maud Montgomery, along with the other books in the Emily series. She felt Emily was just like her because she wanted to be a writer, too. And, like Emily, she began to keep a journal that she wrote and doodled in occasionally.

Although Madeleine may have *hoped* that she wouldn't have to go to school anymore, her parents agreed that her education was important, even if they once again disagreed about what that meant. Out of Madeleine's hearing they argued bitterly. Her mother wanted to send her to the local school, while her father wanted to send her to a boarding school where teachers and students spoke English and where she would get a more formal education. Charles prevailed, as usual.

And so, without Madeleine's knowledge, the decision was made: she was deposited at Châtelard in Montreux, Switzerland, arriving three weeks late, after the "old" girls had reacquainted themselves with each other and the "new" girls had formed their protective cliques. It was torture. Madeleine didn't get along with the other girls or her teachers. She sat alone for her meals in the dining hall, and the first time she took a bath she got in trouble because she stayed in too long and didn't keep her underclothes on—she had never imagined a school could be filled with such strict and extreme rules.

It's no wonder that it took some time for Madeleine to make the best of things during her three years at Châtelard. All the girls were referred to by their number and not their name (which gave Madeleine a lifelong antipathy to bureaucracy and automation), and the school was so poorly heated that the ink in the pens and inkwells froze. Madeleine was also constantly being scolded for being clumsy and forgetful.

Still, she found some things of beauty. In her third year, the window in her room faced Lake Geneva and had an inspiring view of the water and the mountains behind it. Madeleine wrote about it in her journal:

The lake is very lovely just now. The mountains are a purply grey haze, and though the sun is hidden by the grey clouds, there are patches of dull blue sky, and the gold reflection of the sun is on the lake, so bright that it fairly dazzles one to look at.

In New York, she had been unhappy at school but had had her blissful solitary hours of reading and writing in her room at home. At Châtelard, there was no privacy, no chance to be alone, not even in the bathroom, which was monitored by matrons in case anyone took too long. Realizing that she was happiest when she was writing stories, Madeleine learned to retreat into her own world and imagination in the midst of all the noise and distractions. Eventually, she could write anywhere, whether it was her dormitory room or even the classroom, taking her away from her assigned work. Another bright spot was that the girls were allowed to cultivate a small garden plot. She planted poppy seeds, and when they grew she put the flowers under her pillow. She had heard that poppies gave you wonderful dreams.

Whether the poppies were responsible or not, years later she remembered several recurring dreams she had as a young girl. In one, she was an Elizabethan sea captain lying on the deck of her ship, ready to blow it up rather than be

Madeleine,
circa 1933

taken by the Spaniards. In another, she was a woman during World War I, watching her fiancé fly his plane across the horizon. And there were recurring nightmares of war, something she was plagued with her whole life and attributed to her father's war stories.

Eventually, she began to get along better with the other girls. Some became close friends: Pam, Rosy, and Eleanor all corresponded with her through her college years. She found that she loved to ski, that she wasn't as awkward and uncomfortable speeding solo down a mountain as she was playing team sports.

But she remained disorganized, always losing her school tunic or misplacing a book or homework.

Oh diary dear, just must cry to you today. I am so miserable. I can't go skiing because I can't find my things.

And she was not a particularly good student, especially in French and Latin.

I had a vile time in lessons today. In Latin. I hadn't heard something Holmes said, and made a guess at the answers. She blew up and busted, then, and said she had never known anybody take in as little as Hazel and me etc. etc. Then I lost my temper too because I will not be called stupid, and stuck out my jaw and scowled at my book for the rest of the lesson.

Madeleine was also beginning to have trouble with her eyes. She was nearsighted and it was getting worse, and she had flare-ups of iritis, or inflammation of the iris. There was no real cause or cure, but she had to lie in bed and rest,

CHATELARD SCHOOL
MONTREUX

Name _Madeline Camp_ Term _Spring 1932_

Average Age _13 years 4 months_

Form _IVª_

SUBJECT	REMARK	SIGNATURE
		Y. Hopper.
Scripture	Very fair	I. King
English	Madeline can do good work when she takes sufficient care	M.E. Morton
History	Good. She works well and with interest.	
French	Travail quelquefois bon, mais gâté par un grand désordre. Parle plus correctement.	M. Fiaux.
German		
Latin	Very weak. She lacks determination, not ability to learn.	K.E. Holmes.
Mathematics		E.M. Watson
Geometry	must learn to concentrate more in class	Y. Hopper.
Arithmetic	Fair; more concentration needed.	
Science	Could still make much more effort: her work is careless and untidy.	M. Whittaker Smith. E.M. Watson
Geography	Shows interest but more concentration needed	Y. Hopper.
Drill	Fair.	W. Maclaren
Drawing	Has done in good term's work.	W. Maclaren
Dom. Sc.	Crafts. Good. Works with interest.	
Music	Grandes facilités, élève très musicienne qui fera de grands progrès.	H. de Dunand

Next Term begins _April 29ª_ English party leaves London _April 28ª_

Work. Good in some subjects but Madeline must try to make a greater effort over those subjects she finds difficult.

Conduct. Good; improved in many ways but is still too uncontrolled. Y. Hopper

Madeleine's progress reports

CHATELARD SCHOOL
MONTREUX

Name _Madeline Camp_   Term _Spring 1933_

Form _V.b_   Average Age _14 years 5 months_

SUBJECT	REMARK	SIGNATURE
Scripture		
English	Madeline works with enthusiasm but her written work is not always the best she can produce.	I. King
History	Very fair.	J.A.Roberts
French Div.3	A beaucoup de peine à concentrer; travaille quelquefois bien mais de façon trop peu suivie.	M. Giaux
German	Assez bien, doit avoir un peu plus d'assurance	L. Mercanton
Latin	Weak; translation into English sometimes shows intelligence.	K.K.Holmes
Arithmetic	Very fair; Madeline must try not to create unnecessary difficulties	
Mathematics		
Algebra	Very fair	
Geometry	Good work	V. Hopper
Science	Her written work has improved. She has made a real effort to be neater	D. Pompston
Geography		M. Whittaker Smith
Drill	Very fair	
Drawing	Some good & promising work has been done	V. Hopper
Dom. Sc.	Crafts Good. Has worked neatly & well	W. Maclaren
Music	Bien, élève douée	p. Mde Durand

Next Term begins _Friday April 28ᵗʰ_

Work. Very fair sometimes promising. Madeline has worked better this term.

Conduct. Good but Madeline has not yet developed a sense of responsibility with regard to her possessions and punctuality.

V. Hopper.

not allowed to read or write. She spent a great deal of time in the infirmary, which the girls called "the kennel."

She worried about Uncle Bion's children, whom she called "Bébé" and "Poupon": they were often ill, too, and she made paper dolls for them.

> Poor little Poupon has been desperately ill with pneumonia. I got a card from mother today saying that she is better and they are much encouraged. I *do* hope that she will be all right.

By the time Madeleine was in ninth grade, the political climate in Europe was getting more intense—the stock market crash of 1929 had had economic repercussions all over the world, and people were suffering. Totalitarian regimes were on the rise. Adolf Hitler's plans for revitalizing Germany included frightening ideas about racial purity and a climate of political violence created by his Nazi party. He took power in January 1933 and most of Europe was stunned. All of this worried Madeleine's parents, but maybe not as much as the fact that her father hadn't been able to complete a book during the three years they had lived in France. So when Mado's mother became ill, it was the perfect excuse to return home. Home for Madeleine was New York City, but the family would be returning to Jacksonville, Florida: a place she loved to visit, but where she knew she didn't fit in at all.

> I must learn how to dance before I go back. Everybody dances down there. I dance quite a lot with Pam now, but I am not much good yet. I ought to learn to play bridge too, because I believe they play quite a lot down there. But I don't care a darn about playing bridge, I don't want to learn at all.

WHEN I AM (SICK) IN BED

WHEN THEY LIKE ME

Everyone is nice to me when I am ~~sick~~ ill in bed.

All ~~the~~ day long they read to me, and gently rub my head.

But they don't seem to like me much when I an well and strong,

Instead of telling tales to me, they say to "run along."

I wish they loved me then like when I'm sick in bed, but still

It's nicest when I'm well and strong instead of weak and ill.

A poem from Madeleine's journal

Still more troubling was that Charles's health hadn't improved, even in the mountain air. He would be leaving France for humid, sea-level Jacksonville, which was perhaps only marginally better than smoggy, sea-level New York. Charles and Mado's financial situation must have been very precarious for them to decide to depart for Florida and live with Dearma. Still, Madeleine was happy to leave Europe, for rumbles of unrest were beginning. But she also worried about leaving Grandfather Bion, Gaga, Uncle Bion, and her cousins behind with so much talk of war.

More Journal Entries from Châtelard

This morning when we woke up we were all so sleepy that we stayed in bed nearly to the first gong. Pam went out to get her tunic, and I yelled at her to get mine. She brought it in, and then Eleanor found out that she had lost hers. She made an awful fuss, because she didn't know what to do, and when I put on the tunic Pam had brought me, I found out that it was Eleanor's! Then I didn't know what to do. I ran to my closet, and grabbed a tunic and put it on, and I found out that it was Vivian's. I grabbed another tunic just as the second gong went, and luckily that one was mine.

I am getting awfully nearsighted. When I get back to America and have to have my eyes examined I guess that I will have to wear glasses.

It seems with all the banks closing in America that we have been hit pretty badly. That is why I can't go to Montreux for lunch. We can't afford it.

Peggy and I are writing a novel. We don't know the title of it yet, but we know the idea of it, and have started writing it. That is, I have.

I have made a sort of promise to myself saying that I will not read trash books.

Ugh! Exams started today. We had Latin and French. I know that I failed Latin and I have a hunch that I failed French.

Châtelard

Madeleine and Sputzi, Dearma's dog, circa 1935

From Child to Teen

Mado's family had been the center of a scandal when her father, Bion, had left her mother, Caroline, for Gaga some years earlier, because divorce was frowned upon in those days. But Caroline (Madeleine's Dearma) had risen to the occasion, continuing to hold her place in Jacksonville society, splitting her time between a house in the city and an old, rambling beach cottage called Red Gables, which had been built by Dearma's mother, the first Madeleine L'Engle, just a trolley ride away from downtown Jacksonville.

Dearma's beach cottage, Red Gables

When Madeleine and her parents arrived in Florida in the summer of 1933, they found Dearma bedridden at Red Gables, and although it was difficult to see her like that, Madeleine was happy to be at the beach cottage rather than at the house in town. When the cottage had first been built, there was nothing around it for miles. Now it was a last holdout in the midst of a growing amusement park and multiple boardwalks.

Red Gables and the ocean were the two things Madeleine loved about being in Florida. She found the sound of the waves soothing and the swimming enjoyable, especially once she got past the breaking waves to where the Atlantic was smooth and calm. Her morning routine included an early swim, far out to sea. She would let herself float and observe the sky and its changing clouds. Red Gables and the beach had always been important to Madeleine. Her first memory was of being woken up and taken out to look at the stars there, and she would later call that memory her first glimpse of the vastness of the universe—the expanse of the ocean and the star-filled sky.

That fall, when Madeleine was almost fifteen years old, she was sent away to school again, this time to Ashley Hall, a girls' school in Charleston, South Carolina. With glasses. She was nervous. It had taken such a long time for her to become comfortable at Châtelard.

Fortunately, she quickly settled in and found she loved Ashley Hall. She still did miserably in French and Latin, but she adored the principal, Mary Vardrine McBee, who was gifted in bringing out the best in people. Madeleine longed to be in the drama club her first year and was over the moon when she finally got the part of the "second shepherd" in the Christmas play. She went on to get bigger

Ashley Hall

roles—her best one was Sir Andrew Aguecheek in a production of Shakespeare's *Twelfth Night*. She was also encouraged to write original comedies for the club to perform.

The school joined with a local boys' school to hold formal dances, which Madeleine chose to skip.

The first citadel dance is tonight. I did not go. Neither did Polly or Bee. Polly and I ordered some vanilla ice cream and used up our caramel sauce on it. It was grand. We are allowed to stay up until the girls come back from the dance, but I guess I'll go to bed around twelve. They will not be back until one thirty. Hane came in with us and listened to Carol's radio.

Madeleine applied to Ashley Hall's student council, a student group that advised the faculty on disciplinary matters, and on academic and school spirit awards. She was very excited when she learned she had been accepted.

The playbill from the Ashley Hall production of *Twelfth Night*

Tomorrow I am going to be installed. O, diary, I am so happy. I am so thankful that I have been received on student council. Now that I am on the council, I must work hard and try and get on the board.

Being on the student council also conferred privileges, like extended library access, that appealed to Madeleine. The council kept everyone on her toes by having a couple of leadership positions that were rotated and voted on monthly. The highest level of leadership, though, was board member, reserved for upperclasswomen, and the tenure was for a longer term. These positions became a source of anxiety for Madeleine once she was on the student council: the elections for leadership and board were often a popularity contest, and there was a great deal of lobbying and retribution paid, but she did aspire to rise through the ranks.

Madeleine also spent a lot of time writing her own stories and poems.

RED GABLES
JACKSONVILLE BEACH
FLORIDA

SWISS WINTER

I want the snow in my face.
I'm tired of the rain and the sleet.
I want to get on a sled and fly down a hill,
And spend hours climbing up a tall mountain,
        and ski down again in a few minutes.
I want to see the trees with their branches
        laden with snow,
And the Christmas star shining above a tall
        mountain.
I want to hear the scrape of skates on ice,
And the clinking of cups for hot cocoa,
And the wind rushing icily around me.
I want the night sky to be crusted with cold
        stars,
And the window panes to be coated with frost.
I want to have to sleep under woolen blankets
        and quilts,
And to wear warm, comfortable, ski clothes,
And drink bowls of steaming soup,
And get in a sled wrapped in fur robes and
        listen to the bells tinkling on the
        horses harnasses.
I want, 0, how I want a Swiss Winter

Poem, circa 1935

She was very serious about improving her writing and someday being an accomplished author, as shown in a journal entry from the summer after her first year at Ashley Hall.

I am rewriting an old story that I wrote last year called Pippa and hope to make something fairly decent out of it—also, a collection of poems called "Peter Thinks," and when I've finished, I'm going to send it to the publishers. I know that many people get a stage when they want to write, but it is no stage for me. I was born with the itch for writing in me, and o, I couldn't stop it if I tried. I have always written. Why, if I look back to earlier journals I see pages on my desire to write. When I was a tiny child I was never so happy as when scribbling rhymes. O, I have to write, there is no doubt about that, and in this journal as in my first real one, I am going to copy that last wonderful verse from "The Fringed Gentian":

Then whisper, blossom, in thy sleep
How I may upward climb
The alpine path, so hard, so steep,
That leads to heights sublime.
How may I reach that far off goal
Of true and honored fame
And write upon its shining scroll
A woman's humble name.

And now I do swear a vow. I, Madeleine L'Engle Camp, do solemnly vow this day that I will climb the alpine path and write my name on the scroll of fame.

The poem she quotes in this journal entry was reprinted in Lucy Maud Montgomery's Emily series, which remained a favorite of hers. She began writing in her journal in earnest, using it not only to record events but also to sketch characters and practice dialogue.

That summer she went to Huckleberry Camp, in Connecticut, where on one occasion she went too far in playing a practical joke, exercising her storytelling skills but scaring herself in the process.

I wish I did not have a way of doing things that I instantly regret. Tonight I had a devilish—yes, I must use that word—desire to see how gullible Gertie Pike was. So I told her that my name was not really Madeleine Camp, but Carol Grave. Well, it would have been all right if I had let it go at that, but I didn't. I carried it further and said that I was adopted by some Camps, and that before, I had lived in Switzerland with my parents. Well I had to go on then. So I said there was a fire, and I can't write what I said next because it makes me feel too awful, and of course, though Gertie had taken it in I instantly confessed that I had been fooling because it makes me feel awful to think of anything happening to mother and father, and o, I wish I hadn't said it. Supposing it really—O, I can't even think that. O, why did I say it—O, why am I always doing things I feel terribly over after? But I have such an awful way of being and feeling impersonal about myself, and O, I must stop even writing about this or I will worry over it for days.

After camp, she returned home to Red Gables and her parents and Dearma, who was still ill. Days were lazy and hot, and Madeleine worked on a book of poems, wandered the boardwalk, and swam in the ocean. She also thought deeply and continued to be concerned about the state of the world.

I am afraid of ideas tonight. Mother and father talked politics for a couple of minutes tonight, and politics always get me jumpy when the world is in a mess like it is now, and so tonight I am afraid of ideas—not actualities.

An idea has more power over human mind than anything else—actuality you can touch, but ideas are elusive—ununderstandable. But these thoughts have the power to make you understand beauty, fear, rejoice—almost more than actualities.

Madeleine's bedroom was right across from Dearma's. She often had to turn out her light before she was quite ready for sleep in order to not disturb her grandmother, but she didn't mind. She loved the sound of Dearma's gentle snoring. But then, just before Madeleine was scheduled to go back to school, Dearma died.

Dearma died yesterday morning a while before five o'clock. She didn't feel well when she went to bed, and Mother fanned her for a long time. Her pulse was slow, but not as slow as it had been often before. I woke up in the night and heard her go to the bathroom and get back into bed and turn out the light. Later I woke up again and heard her breathing queerly. I ran and told Mother and we called the Doctor but it was too late.

I am not going to remember all that. I am going to remember her the way she really was...The funeral was this afternoon, and O, I can't write anymore. I feel as though my feelings were all bottled up inside me, and I can't take the cork out. I wish I could. It would be such a relief if I could just write everything out...I read in Emily Thinks about the milestones that you pass. I think that this has been my passing from childhood into girlhood, because as mother says, though I am fifteen, I have really been a child all these years.

And I read in another book that a person is never dead until you have forgotten them, so Dearma can never be dead to me, because I will never forget her.

When Madeleine returned to Ashley Hall for her second year of high school, she threw herself into student activities, still excited to be on the student council. She was also elected assistant editor of the school's literary magazine, *Cerberus*.

Cerberus staff photo, with Madeleine standing fourth from left, circa 1936

But her poor grades at Châtelard meant that it was unclear when she would graduate. She had hoped that she would only have another two years of high school, but she was doing poorly in Latin. She found it difficult to put an effort into something she didn't understand or enjoy.

I have just been speaking to Miss McBee about whether I am to graduate next year or the year after. If I pass all five subjects this year, I will be able to graduate next year, but I am so mixed-up in my Latin because of not studying at Chatelard the first year, and being sick a lot of the next year and not studying very hard the rest of it that I am afraid I will fail. Besides, I know so little about it that I am not interested enough to study very hard this year, but Father and Mother want me to learn it because they think it will help me in my writing.

If not obedient, Madeleine was ever creative in her assignments for school. In American history, she wrote a paper on the early American colonies as a series of letters. She imagined a band of dispersed friends writing back to the one who stayed behind in England. She wrote letters from Virginia, Rhode Island, Connecticut, and more. Her teacher, unimpressed, gave her a C+ with this comment: "This is interesting and well done although not what I had expected. History if viewed correctly provides its own thrill and human touch without additional fiction." In English, however, Madeleine's work was so good that she was exempt from taking final exams.

Like most teenagers, Madeleine was caught up in any drama that happened between other girls and herself. She wanted to surround herself with girls who were both effervescent and intellectual, and when she was stuck with someone who wasn't like that, she could be grumpy.

I'd be happier with another roommate. But I don't want to worry Mother and Father. But I don't like Mary. She just gets on my nerves. She has no enthusiasm, no pep or vitality, she hardly ever speaks above a whisper, and she isn't in the least conversational or original or human and she hasn't any backbone. And these are qualities I like in a girl.

Mary and Madeleine never did manage to become friends. Shortly before her sixteenth birthday Madeleine wrote:

But O, I don't want to grow up! I remember how unhappy I was when I was thirteen. I didn't want to be in my teens. I wanted to stay a little girl and I still do.

And once again her father had strong opinions about her education—he thought she needed another year at Ashley Hall.

I am, to put it mildly, discouraged, I have tons of work to make up in Latin and algebra, and so I have to drop one of them. And so just as I am getting interested in old Caesar, I have to put him behind me. Miss McBee says that I can take the Calvert system this summer and make it up, and so graduate next year. So far, well and good, but Father doesn't want me to graduate next year. He thinks 17 is too young. And isn't! O, it isn't! I think eighteen is too old. But I suppose it would help to get a more extensive education, but then I won't graduate from college till I'm twenty-two, and then I want to go to the art students league, and then study abroad, and I'll be middle aged before I finish my education!

Madeleine wrote lots of poetry and sent it to the magazine *Good Housekeeping* under the pseudonym Elizabeth Applegate Martin, her father's grandmother's name, which she thought beautiful. She even wrote a pretend letter to that great-grandmother about it.

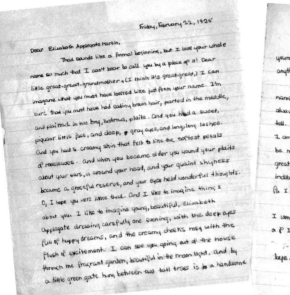

Friday, February 22, 1935

Dear Elizabeth Applegate Martin,

That sounds like a formal beginning, but I love your whole name so much that I can't bear to call you by a piece of it! Dear little great-great-grandmother, (I think it's great-great,) I can imagine what you must have looked like just from your name. I'm sure that you must have had satiny brown hair, parted in the middle, and plaited in two long, lustrous, plaits. And you had a sweet, piquant little face, and deep, # gray eyes, and long, long lashes. And you had a creamy skin that felt to like the softest petals of rose leaves. And when you became older you wound your plaits about your ears, or around your head, and your quaint shyness became a graceful reserve, and your eyes held wonderful thoughts. O, I hope you were like that. And I like to imagine things I about you. I like to imagine young, beautiful, Elizabeth Applegate dressing carefully one evening, with the deep eyes full of happy dreams, and the creamy cheeks rosy with the flush of excitement. I can see you going out of the house through the fragrant garden, beautiful in the moon light. And by a little green gate hung between two tall trees is to a handsome

young man, - great grandfather Martin - waiting, waiting for you! O, anything like that ever happen?

I love your name. Last week I sent two poems under your name to a magazine. They probably won't be accepted, but I shall always try again, whether under your name or not time alone may tell. Perhaps I shall make your name known throughout the world. I am going to try to make some name through me known, whether it be mine a yours or any other. And I know that you wish me luck, great-great-grandmother with the rythmical name. And I'm really indebted to you, for if it wasn't for you I shouldn't be able to try, for I shouldn't be here at all, or at any rate, I wouldn't be me!

I am going to seal this letter up, and someday I shall read it. I wonder if I will be known to the world as Elizabeth Applegate Martin, or P I shall be known to the world at all. Do you know? Can you tell?

And now, good bye; dear Elizabeth Applegate Martin, good bye.

Madeleine L'Engle Camp

When her poems were rejected, she accepted it with good grace and more than a little bit of bravado.

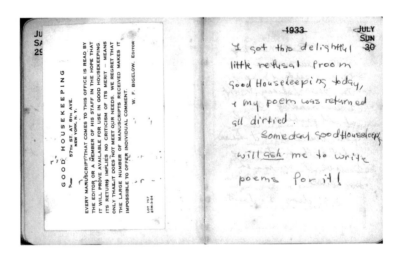

GOOD HOUSEKEEPING
57TH ST. AT 8TH AVE.
NEW YORK, N.Y.

EVERY MANUSCRIPT THAT COMES TO THIS OFFICE IS READ BY THE EDITOR OR A MEMBER OF HIS STAFF IN THE HOPE THAT IT WILL PROVE AVAILABLE FOR USE IN GOOD HOUSEKEEPING. ITS RETURN IMPLIES NO CRITICISM OF ITS MERIT — MEANS ONLY THAT IT DOES NOT MEET OUR NEEDS. WE REGRET THAT THE LARGE NUMBER OF MANUSCRIPTS RECEIVED MAKES IT IMPOSSIBLE TO OFFER INDIVIDUAL COMMENT.

W. F. BIGELOW, EDITOR

-1933-   JULY
              SUN
              30

I got this delightful little refusal from Good Housekeeping today, + my poem was returned all dirtied.

Someday Good Housekeeping will ask me to write poems for it!

She shared her poetry with her parents. Her father would send her back letters of both encouragement and serious feedback.

Saturday, April 20

Darlingest Motherx and Father,

A very happy Easter to you both. I am
sending you copies of some of the poems I have
just written, and I will save the rest to read to
you when I come home next.

NIGHT CRY

The dark trees stretch their arms out and cry.
The moon shivers behind a thin cloud.
The wail of a vessel's horn is heard far out at
                    sea.
The waves crash on the shore under the buffets of
                    the wind
As walls of tall cities fall under the blows of
                    great armies.
The phospherescent glow of the moon that is hid
                    flickers over the wracked
                    earth.
My soul cries out to the lone and desolat beauty,
To the cry of the sobbing night.

NIGHT

The night with its thousands of eyes lies over the
                    earth.
The light from the moon pushes it apart and thrust
And forces a way through in broad silver paths.
The light of the light-ship pierces it with a
                    long, gold, needle.
The street lamps keep it away from them in warm
                    yellow discs.
The headlights of the cars push it aside with
                    rushing streaks of light.
The lights in the windows keep it away from their
                    friendly glow.
The waves brush it aside with their ever dancing
                    lights.
Everything combines to push away the night.

            Please tell me what you think about
these.
            Thank you ever so much for Poetry,
Mother. It was just what I wanted. The first bell
for lunch has rung, so I must stop.
            Loads and loads of love, hugs and
kisses,
                    Madeleine

P.S. I am reading Stalky and Co. again. Don't you
love it. M.

April 21, 1935
Dear Daughter,

    . . . On our way back we stopped at the post-office,
and found your letter with the poems, "Night Cry" and
"Night." I like them both. In the first: "The moon shivers
behind a thin cloud" seems a very suggestive and remember-
able line, but of course all appreciations and criticisms are
personal. Mother thinks that "Night" has too much use of
the word, light, but my feeling is that your intention was to
make your effect with just that repetition, and I believe
with a little smoothing it will be very successful. Of course
"The night with its thousands of eyes—" is in itself very
lovely, and you are perfectly free to phrase it so; but that old
war-horse, "The night has a thousand eyes, the day but one,"
I think detracts from the dignity of your line, because in the
public mind it has much the same appeal as a crooner's
song; but you must decide for yourself. With a little smoothing you have a lovely thing there.

More Journal Entries from Madeleine's First Two Years at Ashley Hall

Tomorrow is Leonora's birthday. She will be seventeen! Heavens! Aren't we aged! Well, I have to wait for two years before I get to be there, anyhow. I wish we didn't have to grow up—at least not so quickly. It is such fun to be a little girl.

We also had forum tonight, and Miss McBee told us of her experiences in the war. It was awfully interesting, but O, I hope that nothing like that ever happens again.

I am much too shy. It is mother's despair! And mine too, incidentally—I hate my shy awkwardness in being introduced to people. Once I get to know them it isn't so bad, and Leonora has often told me that I am a very interesting conversationalist. But I can't be sure of that. It seems to be that I either talk too little or too much.

I must stop losing things, I say things occasionally that I shouldn't say ... Another thing I do occasionally that I hadn't thought of before but that is very serious, and that I must never do again is that when I haven't studied a lesson well enough I exaggerate on the amount I have studied. A lot of people do, but that makes no difference. I haven't been doing it lately because I have been studying, and I didn't realize that I was exaggerating when I did, but it is a form of lying, and I have always prided myself on being strictly honest.

Today I received an autographed copy of *Testament of Youth* by Vera Brittain. Saturday I received a letter from Mr. Brett at Macmillan saying that he had spent a delightful evening with father, and that it was agreed that I would probably enjoy receiving an autographed copy. And it was coming under separate cover and here it is. Everyone says that it is simply wonderful, but I am afraid that it will depress me awfully, because anything about the war always does. O, there mustn't be another war.

O, if only I can succeed and be a poet and author and an artist. I *must*. O, God, give me the *determination*. And the *will to work*, and the *talent*. I wish I dared say genius. I *will* say it. *Please* give me *genius*.

I know italics are midvictorian, and everything else, but when you are as tremendously in earnest as I am, you have to have them.

Louisa May Alcott had an awful temper, and we both have the same birthday. Maybe that has something to do with it! Louisa succeeded, and I must too!

Madeleine, circa 1936

The Eustace Affair

In 1935, at the end of the school year, Madeleine went home for a visit before she went back to Huckleberry Camp. She was pleased to learn that Grandfather Bion and Gaga had moved back to the States and taken up residence in a brand-new skyscraper in Jacksonville. Uncle Bion and his family had stayed in Europe and wouldn't return to Jacksonville until the end of 1940.

After camp that summer, she returned to Ashley Hall in September. Her grades and her father had won the argument: she would be a junior and not a senior that year.

When she found that her friend Bee was going to be her roommate, and that they would have a coveted balcony room, Madeleine was ecstatic. She was elected a board member of the student council, as well as the junior class representative. She was also hoping to be chosen as an honor girl, yet another distinction granted by the Ashley Hall faculty and the student council.

Sometimes I'm going to [be] writing this diary in the third person singular, calling myself what Bee calls me, Scatter. I'm just going to do it whenever I feel like it.

Sunday Scatter's cold was still a cold, and she stayed in bed, propped up on her camp blankets and pillows. She finished *Stalky and Co.* and started another book she had borrowed from one of the new girls called *Swallows and Amazons*. Occasionally, with a little excited shiver she thought about that night, after supper, when the girls who were to be honor girls for the following year would be announced. If only she could be one—but no, she tried not to think about it.

"If I think about it," she thought, "I may get hopeful, and then it will be such a disappointment."

She got up at night for supper and to hear Miss McBee's traditional talk at the first Sunday night of school. When she came, lastly, to the announcements of the honor girls, how they were the ones that were the nearest to what an Ashley Hall Girl should be, she sat calmly. Looking at her lap, hiding the faint hope that might escape from her eyes.

"Here are the honor girls for this year, alphabetically," said Miss McBee's beautiful, calm voice. "Madeleine Camp, Ann McCormick, Judy Penniman, Polly Read."

When Scatter's name was called her face flooded with a happy crimson. She, Scatter, short for Scatterbrains, an honor girl, and all her best friends, Judy, Ann, and Polly honor girls too. And Bee, her best of best friends, would be sure to be one as soon as she had been a boarder long enough.

Her birthday that fall brought up conflicted feelings about growing older.

Well, here I am seventeen! . . . I don't feel a bit older or wiser, but I shall try to act older and wiser.

The student council once again occupied a great deal of Madeleine's time, and she was very involved in the monthly elections and disciplinary hearings of other girls. Much of her journal writing reflects a growing willingness to use the council as a means to judge and punish other students. Lots of girls seemed to have been "called up" before the council for discipline, including Madeleine's friend Cavada Humphrey.

We called Cavada up before the board this afternoon, because she is disregardish of the rules. She may get suspended from Student Council if she isn't very careful. Also several other people. We are going to do rather drastic things about suspending people from Student Council who have proved themselves undesirable, but it's the only thing to do . . . Cavada won't speak to me, and although that fact is very minor, I wonder what under the sun I've done to make her mad. She'll make a great actress probably, but she'll be even more egotistical than most of 'em.

For all Madeleine's concern about the student council, honor girls, and other girls' behavior, she and a group of friends took part in an incident that crossed the line of acceptable behavior: they wrote pretend love letters to another girl at school from a pretend suitor, going as far as to painstakingly doctor postmarks and return addresses.

A very, very beastly thing has happened. Quite a while ago Nancy and I dropped [off] the letters we had written to Edie Bryant by Mr. Eustace Cabot Blake. We had only written two letters. Well, tonight, all on the spur of the moment, we decided to tell her. So we did. So she immediately tells the whole school and poses as an afflicted heroine, and all the unimportant people in school are down on us, and say it was a mean trick, etcetera. I honestly don't think it was mean. The whole thing was done in the spirit of fun, and I think she should have taken it that way and not have been such a lousy sport.

Madeleine eventually lost her defensiveness and came to regret her part in the "Eustace affair." She worried that it would impact the next student council vote. As it turned out, she didn't lose her place on the council, but she did lose the honor of being on the board. Someone else was also elected for junior class representative, and that was a blow.

I helped count the votes, and it was awfully hard to just act funny when I saw her getting more votes than I. I think I was too sure about the affair of the letters; maybe it wasn't that, but if it wasn't, what was it. I thought I had improved, and I thought I was better than Ruthie. If I know, and I do, that my character hasn't deteriorated, I shouldn't let it hurt me, but it does. I still have a chance to get on again from the elections by the whole school, and oh, I don't know what I'll do if I don't, for I couldn't bear to go home next week end and tell Mother and Father. About the hardest thing of all was congratulating Ruth; I beamed and said, "Oh, Ruthie, I'm so glad; I'm so glad," and had an awful time not showing that I wanted to cry. It was a lie, of course, to say that, because how could I be glad when I have evidently lost the respect of Student Council, but at least it made me feel more self respecting than if I hadn't said anything about it, and had rushed off somewhere to cry. And I can't talk to anybody about it, not even to Beetles, because I won't show how it hurt.

Madeleine worked hard to put the Eustace affair behind her, but it shadowed the rest of her junior year and caused her a great deal of pain.

Journal entries from before and after the Eustace affair show that Madeleine was very serious about her work, and had started to examine her own self and who she was. She felt that she had different kinds of moods and that those moods needed to have different names, because to her they felt like distinct personalities. She could be "Diana Masterson," who was a bit reckless and enthusiastic; "Daphne Parish," who liked to spend her time painting and writing poetry; or, again, "Elizabeth Applegate Martin," who observed and empathized, and took the sorrows of the world on her shoulders. She was also "Madeleine L'Engle."

She is the dramatic part of me—the part of me that longs to act—the one that acts even when there is no audience. The me that often comes just anytime, and almost always after hearing a wonderful piece of music, reading a good book, or seeing a grand play or movie.

I can't explain all these things. These aren't the only me's. There is a me that is none of these things that I am in between lives that, perhaps, even more inexplicable than they. And there are other roads besides, but these, I think, are the ones that occur oftenist.

Madeleine's exploration of personalities combined with her desire to be a writer, and she began work on a novel.

I wrote quite a bit on my book about Anne and Diana and Daphne and the rest yesterday. I think it's fairly good. It isn't an ordinary boarding school story with violently exciting plot and impossible characters. It is real people and real events. To people who are at boarding school, it is really the most important part of their life. They have to learn to live with other people and adjust themselves in a complete little world.

As her literary ambition grew, Madeleine started to seek advice from established writers and critics. She sent some poems to Archibald Rutledge, the poet laureate of South Carolina.

He doesn't like my subjects or free verse, he says my subjects aren't poetic, and he thinks free verse is fast being outmoded. I think subjects are a matter of taste, and I disagree about free verse, but he did say something awfully nice at the end. He said that I saw things with a poet's eye, and that there was no doubting my ability, and that one needs to suffer to write really great poetry, and that if I suffer I may really get somewhere. I am not willing to suffer to write mediocre poetry, but I am to write really great poetry, and I will be great!—although magazines still continue to send me discouraging rejection slips.

More Journal Entries from Madeleine's Third Year at Ashley Hall

When Scatter went out for anything she always went thoroughly, and now in much of her spare time she went over and practised her Bach Prelude. It was really worth hours of practising, and getting violently excited over; it always left her with a feeling of exhilaration, and a vast amount of energy.

We discussed the girls who sent in applications today. Quite a few were passed that I didn't think should be, but I don't expect the faculty will pass them.

Hope this year 1936 brings peace and not war. Oh, if only it can. War would be too horrible. I do hope that this year can be a good year, as good to me as 1935. 1935 was awfully good to me. Representative at Board, Board member, Sir Andrew in Shakespearean play, those 2 weeks with Bee and Maggie, camp, cup at end of camp, school, rooming with Bee on balcony, Honor Girl.

Am at Woodford's table again this week. It's really awfully luck. Last week although I was at her table no one talked much, and this week I'm afraid Faith and I carry it to the other extreme discussing politics, diplomacy, etcetera. Woodford really got rather annoyed at lunch, but I do so love to argue and Faith is an excellent opponent. It wouldn't be so bad if we didn't raise our voices when we got excited.

MADELEINE L'ENGLE CAMP
New York, New York

Entered '33   Purple

"My library was dukedom large enough."
—Shakespeare

Student Council; Representative of Student Council, '34-'35; Student Council Board, '35-'37; Treasurer of Student Council Board, '36; Vice-President of Student Council Board, '36; President of Student Council Board, '37; President of Student Council House Board, '36, '37; Le Verre D'Eau, '36, '37; Dramatic Club, '35-'37; Christmas Play, '34,-'37; Shakespearean Play, '34-'37; Madrigal Club, '36; Cerberus Staff, '34, '35; Editor of Cerberus, '35-'37; French Club, '33-'36; Vice-President French Club, '35, '36; Athletic Association, '33-'37; Purple Basketball Team, '36; Riding Club, '33-'37; Dance Group, '36-'37; President of Junior Class, '35-'36; Senior Privileges; Poetry Prize, '36.

Ashley Hall senior yearbook picture, 1937

Senior Year

In the summer of 1936, instead of going to camp, Madeleine stayed in Jacksonville to take a college entrance exam preparatory class. She was thinking about her future. She knew, of course, that she was going to be a writer, but she wasn't sure college needed to be part of it. But Miss McBee, the Ashley Hall principal, often took a special interest in some of her students and encouraged them, including Madeleine, to go to Smith College, her own alma mater. It was considered a great honor to be tapped by Miss McBee, and Madeleine knew it. That, and her father's approval of the idea, inspired her to try to prepare for the exam.

During the class she met Patricia Collins, who was, like Madeleine, an unusual girl among the southern students. She, too, was very tall, gawky, and bookish, and she wanted to study medicine. Madeleine and Patricia developed a fast and true friendship that lasted the rest of their lives. Like another of Lucy Maud Montgomery's characters, Anne Shirley, the protagonist in *Anne of Green Gables*, Madeleine recognized "kindred spirits" and knew they were precious.

In Jacksonville, Madeleine was expected to attend social dances and aspire to genteel southern womanhood. She did not. She hated the dances and did not harbor the expected aspiration. She was not good at small talk, she was awkward with the boys (most of whom she towered over), and she inevitably threw up at every dance. She would find out later that she was allergic to bivalves: the scallops and clams and oysters that were southern staples in various forms at the dances. But at the time she felt as if she were allergic to the life that her parents hoped her to have. She became expert at finding excuses to stay off the dance floor; dawdling in the bathroom so no one would ask her to dance and even going so far as to rip her dress on purpose so she would have to stay home and sew it up.

Madeleine, circa 1937

When she returned to Ashley Hall in September 1936, she was a senior, rooming with her friend Nancy. She was still on the student council, but she wasn't elected to the board until another girl left. With that, she felt the Eustace affair of the previous spring was finally behind her, and she was full of energy and excitement.

Then came the bad news: her father was desperately ill. He had caught a cold that turned into pneumonia. He was in the hospital in Jacksonville, and Madeleine needed to come at once to say goodbye. As she sat on the train, she tried to read *Jane Eyre*, but she couldn't concentrate. Instead she looked out the window, watching the familiar landscape and saying over and over again: "Please, God, do whatever is best for Father. Please, do whatever is best."

He died on October 30, before she arrived. Everyone was sad and somber, but there were no tears, not even from Mado, who simply went quiet, a paragon of stoic virtue.

Madeleine was raised to believe that such stoicism was the ideal. A journal entry written after her return to Ashley Hall indicates her effort to mask her emotional turmoil.

It is very hard to write this without crying, but I hope I have been brave. I didn't want to cry—not really cry—when I was in Jax because I wanted to be brave and to help mother, and when I got back to school the tears wouldn't come, but there was a great ache, and it was hard to laugh and joke, but I tried, and I hope succeeded fairly well.

Her father was on her mind a great deal in the following months, and his death pricked her ambition.

One reason that I don't spend as much time on my lessons as I should is that when I think of a poem I simply have to write it, and I have ideas for so many poems and stories too often. But I do think that writing poetry and stories, and reading books in my free time instead of studying is far more valuable to me than if I did study. For I have to succeed in my writing, for Father's sake as well as my own, for it meant so much to him, and he just missed success by bad fortune and not enough discipline.

In 1936, higher education for women wasn't a given. Madeleine would be able to finish high school at Ashley Hall, but now that her father was gone, it was expected that she would return to Jacksonville and take care of her mother instead of going to college.

I do want to go to college, but I can't leave Mother alone next year, and whatever I do, I must never let her think that it is a sacrifice for me to give college up. But I do want to go. One thing—most of the greatest writers never went to college. Oh, I must, I will succeed!

Although Madeleine thought her journal writing was an important outlet, one of her teachers thought differently.

Miss Sylvia says she doesn't approve of diaries because she thinks that they are always written with the thought of other people's seeing them and having them published, and that one is never honest with oneself in them.

Now, to be perfectly honest with myself, I am writing this journal with the idea of having it published, but not until I'm dead. Because I think we're living in a very interesting age, and the thoughts and impressions of any young girl of average intelligence and interests of things more than the commonplace should possibly prove valuable historically in understanding the people of a certain period. And I'm always trying more and more to be perfectly honest with myself, although I absolutely admit that I wasn't at first, though not putting down all things often put me in an unfavourable rather than a favourable light. But now I'm trying to put the bad things about myself as well as the good. What are my faults? Well, I'm very untidy, except where my art is concerned [...] I do try to be neat, but so often I stop to write just a bit more of that poem or read just one more paragraph when I should be cleaning up. I have a sharp temper, and I lose it easily, but I don't stay mad long and I never sulk. I worry too much, and I have too many moods. I ask too much of people. When I am interested in a conversation I am apt to talk too much, but I don't think I burble about trivialities. I don't study hard enough. There are many more things, I'm sure, but I can't think of them just now. As for my virtues—I'll leave them for the observant reader to find out!

The Christmas holidays that year were bittersweet. Mado had sold Red Gables, but she had moved into an apartment in the new skyscraper in Jacksonville where Grandfather Bion and Gaga had settled, so Madeleine and Mado did have family to keep them company.

Back at school, Madeleine was elected president of the student council for the spring 1937 term, the highest honor, but after all the drama and heartache, she didn't find much joy in the position.

The day after tomorrow the Easter hols begin! I need them very much. Being president of Student Council is very wearing, and it is such a bore being an "example" all the time. I don't feel the joy in being prominent that I did when I was "coming up" in the world. I hope I'm not as smug about it all as I was then. I'm more popular now at any rate, I think most people like me now instead of just my own particular crowd of friends. At any rate, I haven't any particular enemies—except for Miss Thomas. That woman!

Later that spring, she worried about her final exams.

The exams begin next week, and I'm petrified, especially of chemistry. It would be just too awful if I failed and didn't graduate after having gone through these four years to do so. And if I don't do well on the school exams, what chance have I with college boards? Although it seems awfully futile taking college boards when I'm not going to be able to go to college.

Despite her worries, Madeleine did graduate from Ashley Hall. In her senior yearbook she was described this way:

Known For: Chemical fantasy, Admired For: Literary ability, Main Occupation: Falling down, Ambition: To stand on two feet, Likely to Be: First woman president.

But it still wasn't clear whether or not she would be going to college. Her grades, her family obligations, and her family's financial situation all seemed to threaten.

about it showed us about it. What intrigued Dobie, Jimmy, and I the most were two lamps made out of the water-works system of a camel. Believe it or not, they really made lovely lamps when they were lighted. After we had finished at Walmer we set out for Dover Castle. It was frightfully windy there, and all our hats kept blowing off. I didn't think it was nearly as interesting there as at Walmer. They meet there for the Fox Hunts. Dobie is meant to be the best horse-woman in that locality. Jimmy says she usually falls off at the jumps and everybody always gets ready to pick her up. When we had finished looking at Walmer we went back to Sandwich Bay.

Sandford, where they had another room for us, as their new house isn't ready yet, and their old cottage has no guest room. We were told not to dress for dinner, so we just fixed our hair and went over to "Fanny." The Vicars dining

The Vicars darling, awfully nice, and also poor Mr. ____ been in bot. made him first won't talked night times

BALALAIKA

angela Wischer, the terribly typical, but awfully nice man, Sibbeth who has South America a Dobie says I quite a lot with as he is usually fully shy and I say a word, but he to me a lot all that and all the other we saw him, and Dobie told me that one morning he started telling her how sweet he thought I was! I liked Old Sib frightfully, too. After Dinner, Sib, Dobie, Jimmy, angela, and I drove to Sandwich and went to the movies — We go again to the movies — the program, which I had already seen, but I didn't mind seeing it again

as it is really awfully good. When we stood up to sing "God Save The King" at the end, we suddenly noticed that we were the only people in the theatre! It was awfully funny. While we were driving back to Sandwich Bay we stopped to watch the searchlights. There are several military camps near here, and at night they often practise sighting the airoplanes. Great shafts of light crawled about the sky, and when they sighted a plane, the plane looked like some shape silver bird!

It is quite late, so I must stop and go to bed now. But then will I catch up with myself. I have so much that I want to write, and so very little time to write.

Illustration from Madeleine's journal

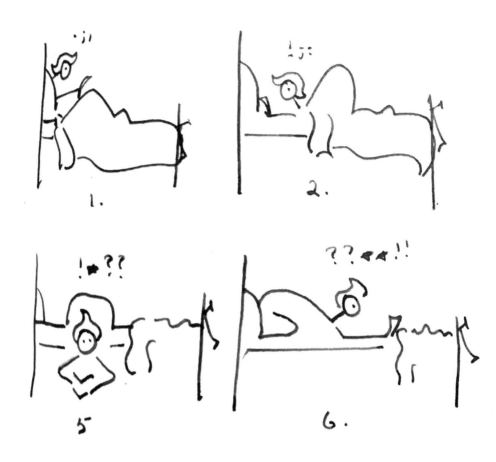

More Journal Entries from Madeleine's Senior Year at Ashley Hall

I'm so desperately, *desperately* glad I'm young. Growing old isn't so bad if you can only do it gracefully, but so many people do it in such a sloppy manner that [it] is almost repulsive.

We had a perfectly horrible Chemistry test yesterday, which, thank goodness, I passed, thanks to a couple of lucky guesses. It is a great comfort to remember that Kipling was terrible in Latin and Maths!

EXAMS ARE COMING

Illustration from Madeleine's journal

I am longing for a letter from Peggy to give me the English point of view [on Edward VIII's abdication in December 1936]. Poor Woodford is very cut up about it. Miss McBee says that Edward would not have made a good king—that his character, although charming, is weak; and that he drinks terribly, and I know only too well what that means.

Madeleine, circa 1938

The College Years

In the summer of 1937, after her high school graduation, Madeleine and her mother went on a trip together. Madeleine still didn't know what she would be doing in the fall, but it didn't seem to bother her too much.

What a thrill it is to get on a train with no definite idea of how long one is to be gone, or where one is to go, even if the first part of the journey is over very familiar land . . . College Boards are over, but whether or not they are passed I can't say yet; and I have the summer and the world ahead of me!

Mado and Madeleine spent several days in New York City with old friends who took them to the theater and concerts. Mrs. O, with whom Madeleine had corresponded over the years, visited, too, and Madeleine was very happy to see her. On July 9, Madeleine and her mother set sail for England and France, where they would visit family and some of their old haunts. Madeleine also seemed to have gotten over her aversion to dancing.

I danced quite a bit with the ship's doctor last night. He is an awfully good dancer. I danced with him and another man whose name I don't know—and he was introduced to me!—this evening, but mainly with the doctor. He tried to kiss me, but otherwise he was all right. We had balloons and it was all very gay.

Madeleine and Mado had a good time in London, but at the end of July, when Madeleine found out that she had been accepted to Smith, she started to have a wonderful time. Smith wouldn't start until the end of September. Mado selflessly insisted that she attend. Madeleine knew it would be difficult to leave her mother and live in faraway Massachusetts, but her experience at boarding schools had made her independent. She knew she was ready.

Madeleine,
circa 1939

She liked Smith. Her friend Cavada Humphrey from Ashley Hall was also there, and during her first year she made new friends and enjoyed her classes. As at Ashley Hall, Madeleine and all her friends had nicknames for each other. For her time at Smith, Madeleine was referred to as "Tony."

There was sadness, too, not only at being so much farther away from her mother than she had been at Ashley Hall, but also at missing her father, especially on her birthday.

Today I am nineteen. I feel very, very old, and also very immature and adolescent... There was nothing from Father. Last year at my birthday I was still numb—I didn't quite realize things yet—and I was with mother and there were so many things from everybody that I didn't really miss him so much on this particular day—Oh, Father—

Her journal writing slowed down considerably in college, but she wrote daily postcards to her mother.

Madeleine's postcards to her mother

February 2, 1938

Mum darling,

The English exam is tomorrow and I do hope I can get a decent mark in it. Oh! but I'll be relieved when it's over and I'll be all through! This Sunday I'll really write you a letter.

It's the most wonderful weather—cold and crisp. We've been going on nickle walks for our exercise. You know—at each corner you flip a nickle—heads left, tails right. It's lots of fun and we've got to some awfully queer out of the way places. Must stop now and get back to the Elegy, which is where I am at this point. —M.

When she did write in her journal, often during frequent trips to the infirmary with a cold or flu, she wrote about her past, describing what life had been like at Châtelard or at

Ashley Hall, or she wrote character sketches of other young women at Smith. She also had class papers to do, and she worked on her stories and poems. Still, she made observations in her journal about writing.

I made a discovery yesterday. I don't suppose it's an original sort of discovery at all, but at any rate, I found it for myself. When you write anything—a poem or a story—it's yours only as long as only you know anything about it. As soon as anybody reads it, it becomes partly theirs, too. They put things into it that you never thought of, and they don't see many things that you thought plain.

Her short stories were often based on incidents in her own life, moments when she had an epiphany or had to resolve some kind of conflict. She wrote about that Christmas vacation from Châtelard that she would continue to revisit throughout her life, when her parents were wrapped up in their own worries and sadness. When Mado read the short story Madeleine proudly showed her, Madeleine was shocked when Mado burst into tears. Madeleine hadn't realized how much she had been able to capture in her writing, and it gave her her first inkling that her writing knew more than she did.

She met professors at Smith who helped her hone her craft and whose lessons remained with her throughout her life. Esther Cloudman Dunn taught Shakespeare and drove home the powerful thought that the playwright always started with an attention-getter: a storm, a battle, a fistfight. Professor Dunn also confessed that there was one Shakespearean play she had never read because she couldn't bear to have read all of his works.

Another professor, Mary Ellen Chase, taught the novel. On the first day of the survey class she handed out a one-hundred-question quiz about *Jane Eyre* with questions like "What color dress was Jane Eyre wearing when she met Mr. Rochester?" Indignant, Madeleine turned the page over and wrote: "I don't know what color the dress was, but I know what the book is about." She then wrote an essay instead of taking the quiz. Professor Chase handed the quiz back to her with the remark "Take no more quizzes."

Professor Chase, in a college-wide address, once divided all works of literature into three categories, "major, minor, and mediocre." Her New England accent made it sound like "majah, minah, and mediocah," and that phrase became a running joke on campus. But it wasn't entirely a laughing matter for Madeleine or her classmates. They all aspired to being "majah" and feared being judged "mediocah."

Leonard Ehrlich taught creative writing, and although Smith would allow only one creative writing class to be taken for credit, Madeleine studied with him multiple semesters, not caring about the credit. He encouraged her and thought she had great promise as a writer. Hearing his words, she felt both vindicated—"I do have talent!"—and terrified—"What if I can't live up to his expectations?" But under Professor Ehrlich's tutelage she wrote many short stories, some of which were published in Smith's literary journals, and some of which she reworked later into scenes in her novels.

She didn't respond positively to all her writing teachers: when one commented with a Freudian interpretation on a story of hers, she dropped the course.

She met Marie Donnet and they became best friends.

Madeleine and Marie, circa 1939

They were both active in the theater department. Marie was an actor and director, and in some ways the opposite of Madeleine: outgoing, confident, and charismatic. They seemed to bring out the best in each other, and they accomplished a great deal on campus. Together, they started French House (a French-speaking dormitory), produced multiple plays, and had dreams of moving to New York together and making their mark on the theater. While

Madeleine mostly concentrated on writing, she was also happy to take small parts onstage. Marie had much more of a stage presence, and Madeleine was as captivated with her as everyone else was. In turn, Marie was steadfast in her support of Madeleine as a writer.

Madeleine was active in various student publications, reviving the campus literary magazine, *Opinion,* and then editing the *Smith College Monthly.* A classmate and colleague named Bettye Goldstein was also on the staff of both publications. Bettye later became famous as Betty Friedan, author of the feminist classic *The Feminine Mystique.*

Madeleine adapted some of her short stories into plays, and was constantly revising and reenvisioning her work. Both Madeleine and Marie were determined to be, as Professor Chase would say, a "majah" force in the theater. Marie had met Eva Le Gallienne, founder of New York's Civic Repertory Theatre and the most famous actress and director of the day, and found there was a chance that Miss LeG (as everyone referred to her) would come to Smith to direct a student play. Marie sent her Madeleine's play *A Weekend in the Country*. Although the visit fell through, Miss LeG encouraged Marie and Madeleine to look her up when they moved to New York City after college.

Eva Le Gallienne, circa 1930–40

Marie and Madeleine were giddy with excitement. They made plans to have Miss LeG produce Madeleine's next, and better, play on Broadway.

Madeleine, circa 1941

The Best School for a Writer

When Madeleine graduated from Smith College in 1941, the world news was beyond frightening. Hitler had invaded several countries, and Europe was being devastated by World War II. Madeleine feared that the United States would soon have to join the Allies in order to end it.

Yet her own future was bright—not only were Madeleine and Marie moving to New York City, but several of their friends from the drama department at Smith, including Cavada Humphrey, were hoping to make their way to Broadway as well. Madeleine's dear friend Patricia Collins from Jacksonville would be in the city, too—she was starting medical school at Columbia University.

Before settling in the city, however, Madeleine and Marie spent that summer in Cape May, New Jersey, acting in a summer-stock theater company.

Madeleine, circa 1941

Afterward, they moved to an apartment on West Ninth Street, right in the heart of Greenwich Village. The neighborhood had a colorful reputation as a home to artists, both starving and successful. Madeleine was going to write plays and fiction, plus do a little acting on the side in an effort to understand character and dialogue (she would later say that the theater was the best school for a writer), and Marie was also going to try out for parts in plays so that she could work her way up the theatrical production ladder and eventually become a director. They both felt that Marie was the one who could quite possibly become a star.

The move to New York was a big one. Mado tried to discourage Madeleine. Going to college so far away from home was one thing, but a precarious start as a writer in the big city was another. Her mother understood and accepted that Madeleine was a writer—she had married one, after all—and knew that it was imperative for Madeleine, as it had been for Charles, to write. But couldn't she do it in Florida?

Madeleine would not be deterred. Knowing that if she pushed too hard it might cause irreparable harm to their relationship, and wanting to make sure her daughter would live comfortably, Mado offered Madeleine some furniture that had been in storage all these years from the apartment on East Eighty-Second Street, including the parlor grand piano. Mado also provided some financial help, with the condition that a bedroom in the apartment be available to her whenever she visited. However, Mado didn't make the trip much more than once a year.

Madeleine's beloved Mrs. O was back in the picture—she didn't have a telephone but was available as a maternal figure for Madeleine, and was hired by Mado to sew curtains and check in on Madeleine every now and again.

Dear Mrs. Camp,

I received your letter and check. Many thanks for same. Your letter sounded as if you were very depressed. I know you are greatly worried over Madeleine and her future. Sometimes I feel myself it's too bad she chose such a hard profession for I think it's a very hard one. I have not heard from Madeleine in a couple of weeks, I did have a neighbour call up last week and ask how she was and she answered and said she was very well and would write to me. So far I have not heard from her. I know she had a cold around the holidays for May called up and she told her. I can't understand Marie's mother writing to you and complaining for after all I think your position is much worse for she can see Marie and you are so far away from Madeleine. I know at the present time they are taking up with Miss Le Gallienne and have no time for anyone. I only hope and trust to God she will have the right influence over her. Do you know anything about her, if she is a fine character? Young people are so easy taken in and now is the time to lay her foundation for the future.

Mrs. Camp, don't feel Madeleine doesn't think about you and I really feel she does hold things back from you so as you won't worry. I have told her time and again to keep you posted all the time with what she is doing . . . I think Marie's mother resents Marie having no time for her only for Madeleine and she expected when she would live so near she would see more of her and she don't and that's where the trouble comes in.

Mary O'Connell

Even so, her mother worried, a lot. In response, Madeleine continued to write daily postcards.

March 21, 1942

Mummy darlingest,

If we didn't keep always the intensity of dreaming we have when we're children we couldn't even write or act or paint or compose or play or whatever it is we do. It makes things harder for us, yes—but it also makes them better. If we're more unhappy than other people we're also more happy—I wish you could understand that—it would keep you from worrying about lots of things.

Loads and loads of love, hugs, & kisses—

Madeleine.

But Mado wanted more details than could be put on a postcard, so she cajoled her daughter in multiple ways to be more in her confidence. But after years of being regimented and rule-bound in boarding school and college, Madeleine decided no one was going to tell her what to do or when to do it. For the first time, she was independent and she loved it! She and Marie had a rotating band of roommates, and while she had often chafed at the rules at school, she quickly saw the wisdom of having some guidelines when living with a group of people. She hated doing the dishes but discovered she loved cooking, so that became her job.

Madeleine wrote and sent out stories to magazines and periodicals. She spent some money seeing plays (seats at the top row of the balcony often sold for one dollar). She taught English and writing to European refugees. And when the United States entered the war in December 1941, after Pearl Harbor, she, like everyone else, swallowed her fear of the violence on her doorstep by taking Red Cross training and volunteering in the newly formed American Theatre Wing, which sponsored programs to help the Allies in the war. One of the programs was selling war bonds at different plays being performed throughout the city. An unexpected perk of this was being able to see lots of plays for free: after the lobby emptied, the volunteers were allowed to stand in the back of the theater or sidle into an empty seat.

Through Marie and her work with the Theatre Guild (a production company and incubator of talent), the two friends cultivated a cohort of like-minded, ambitious theater people, including Herbert Berghof, an actor who had left Vienna, Austria, in 1938. He later became a renowned acting teacher whose students included Jon Stewart, Al Pacino, Liza Minnelli, Robert De Niro, and Matthew Broderick. Berghof was older than Madeleine, worldly and successful, and his interest in Madeleine was flattering and intoxicating. There was flirtation, too.

Madeleine had always been shy and awkward in her romantic life, so she wondered but never asked if he was married. (He never said!) They talked mostly about art and work, and she thought Berghof was fascinating and sweet and earnest.

Starstruck and ambitious, and spurred on by Eva Le Gallienne's casual offer to be in contact when they came to New York, Madeleine and Marie were obsessed with getting a play of Madeleine's into her hands. That play was a drama called *Ilse*, and they were convinced it was the perfect vehicle for Miss LeG's talents, because to them *Ilse* was the perfect heroine, full of honor and tragedy.

After Marie sent the play to Miss LeG in the spring of 1942, they were on tenterhooks waiting for her reply. Would Miss LeG understand the play and the character? Would she agree to work with them and do *Ilse* as her next project? Madeleine was aware of the audacity of their request, but she also had complete faith that the play was good and that it was right for Miss LeG.

But then they heard that Miss LeG had been hospitalized with pneumonia. Madeleine careened from worry about her play to worry about Miss LeG, whose genius and illness, she thought, were like her own father's.

In spite of her anxiety, Madeleine kept working on rewriting and workshopping *Ilse* with her theater friends. And she couldn't stop fantasizing about what it would be like to work with Miss LeG. But when Miss LeG recovered, Madeleine learned she was starting a new project—*Uncle Harry*, by a playwright named Thomas Job—and that she wouldn't be directing the play, but starring in it. Margaret Webster, who was best known for her productions of Shakespeare, would be directing it, and she was one of Marie's idols. Madeleine was plunged into despair because it meant Miss LeG wouldn't be doing *Ilse*.

However, she soon rallied. Miss LeG hadn't responded to *Ilse* yet—maybe that meant she hadn't even read it? Marie and Madeleine knew they had to be persistent and lucky as well as talented in order to get their big break, so they arranged to sell their American Theatre Wing bonds at a play called *Angel Street*, which was being performed in a theater close to the Broadhurst Theatre, where *Uncle Harry* was in rehearsals. They made friends with the Broadhurst's doorman, Bill, who was an old vaudevillian. He was very happy to show two eager young fans backstage after hours. Once they even had a picnic with Bill on the stage!

Madeleine and Marie stalked the theater after work in the weeks leading up to the opening of *Uncle Harry*, hoping to see Miss LeG and hear what she thought about *Ilse*, but they didn't have any luck. They also heard rumors that Miss LeG and Margaret Webster were going to start a theater company if the reviews of *Uncle Harry* were good. This

Uncle Harry playbill

meant that the play would be able to move to a bigger theater and then go on tour—it also meant that Miss LeG could be tied up with *Uncle Harry* for as long as two years. The good news for Madeleine and Marie was that if the theater company happened, they could audition for apprenticeships and, if accepted, work full-time on the production, gaining valuable experience and exposure while playing small stage roles.

Once *Uncle Harry* opened, Madeleine saw it several times that first week and thought it was decent, but in no way worthy of Miss LeG's talents.

And there was still no news about *Ilse*. Being so near Miss LeG for weeks without being able to speak to her was almost too much to bear, and time was running out—it was June 1942, and Madeleine and Marie had signed on with a summer-stock company and were getting ready to leave the city. Forced into action the day they were to depart for the summer, Marie sent a note backstage after the matinee performance asking to see Miss LeG. She was overjoyed when Miss LeG's maid came to the door and asked her to please come back after the evening performance. But when the young women returned that night, the maid seemed not to even recognize Marie. "Miss Le Gallienne isn't seeing anyone tonight," the maid said. "If you have anything important to say, you can write it down."

They were crushed, but they hurriedly composed a letter from Marie asking Miss LeG not to read her copy of *Ilse*, if she hadn't already, because there was a new version that was much better.

Dear Miss Le Gallienne — ~~Please forgive the appearance~~ paper — I's ~~all I have at the moment~~ ~~of this note but~~ just wanted to see you tonight to ask you please not to read the ~~script~~ play by Madeleine L'Engle Camp which we sent you ~~the~~ Several important changes have been made ~~in~~ ~~by last act~~ + naturally the author ~~is very anxious~~ would like ~~to~~ have you ~~read~~ the revised version — Of course we know you must be flooded with scripts right now & there isn't much of danger of your picking it up, but because there ~~is a~~ is a chance that you might, we wanted to ~~tell~~ you not to ~~as quickly as~~ possible — If you ~~don't want to read it at all~~ ~~reading it~~ if you ~~just~~ ~~aren't interested~~ ask your secretary to send us a note & we won't bother you with it — I suppose it would have been simpler if I'd written ~~to~~ you about it in the first place but I did want to see you — ~~Again~~ Please ~~excuse~~ forgive the appearance of this note ~~but~~ I am writing standing in the middle of the street — Sincerely ~~Anne~~ Yvonne

Rough draft of letter to Eva Le Gallienne

Dear Miss Le Gallienne—

Please forgive the paper—it's all I have at the moment—I just wanted to see you tonight and ask you please not to read the play by Madeleine L'Engle Camp which we sent you. Several important changes have been made and naturally the author would like you to read the revised version—of course we know you must be flooded with scripts right now and there isn't much of a danger of your picking it up, but because there is a chance that you might, we wanted to tell you not to as quickly as possible—if you don't want to read it at all just ask your secretary to send us a note and we won't bother you with it—I suppose it would have been simpler if I'd written to you about it in the first place, but I did want to see you—Again, please forgive the appearance of this note. I am writing standing in the street.

Gratefully yours, Marie Donnet

Marie heard back from Miss LeG, who said it was fine to drop off the new version at the theater. Madeleine and Marie left shortly thereafter to spend the summer at the Straight Wharf Theatre on Nantucket, an island off the coast of Massachusetts. Miss LeG wrote to them, saying that she was interested in the play but still felt there was something not quite right about the ending. She ended the letter saying that Madeleine "must go on writing." Madeleine, ecstatic, copied the letter from Miss LeG into her own letter to her mother.

June 28, 1942

Mother darlingest,

What do you think of this? Read it several times. Carefully. We still feel hopeful. [Miss LeG] is famous for not doing things just to be kind, and why would she and [Margaret] Webster be willing to see me in the autumn if they didn't think I could do something with Ilse? What do you think? (Don't show this to anybody.) . . . Well, darling, what do you think? Tell me honestly.

Loads and loads of love, hugs, and kisses, Madeleine

Madeleine was exhilarated. She continued with her small acting parts in summer stock and began work on a comedy, *'Phelia*. Marie sent Miss LeG Madeleine's third revision of *Ilse*, and the two friends felt sure they would hear from her once they returned to New York.

But they were bitterly disappointed each day that passed with no word. Madeleine was supposed to go to Jacksonville for a visit—her mother had broken her leg earlier in the summer, and Madeleine's absence from her mother's side was noted by the extended family. But she didn't want to leave New York. They argued.

September 25, 1942

Darling sweet,

Let us get a few things straight at once. I haven't written you that I want to come to Jax, because you are quite right, I don't want to. But I do want to see you—and it's because I want so to see you, rather than the sense of obligation (that I do have) that I'm coming right now. Because you see, sweet, this is a very bad time to leave New York. Everything is going on. Not just waiting to hear from Miss Le Gallienne, although that, I admit, is a large part of it. I've had a chance to work in a semi-professional group in Ibsen's "John Gabriel Borkman" which I had to turn down because of not being here. I almost got a regular equity

company that is doing "Stage Door" on the Subway Cir-
cuit. If I'd got that I couldn't have afforded to turn it
down. You see, darling, these are the reasons I don't want
to leave just now. Do you understand? And these are the
reasons why I can't stay as long as I'd like to otherwise.
But I do want to see you, more than I can tell you. I
thought you understood that. You musn't ever think that
you have been weighed in the balance and found wanting.
You are over-weight [that is, more important], if anything.
We poor artists are famous for being misunderstood by
our families, and I am perpetually thankful that I have a
mother who is as understanding as you are. And when I
look at the parents of many of my friends I can think
gladly "I need never be ashamed to have my mother meet
my friends." I hate so to have you unhappy about me, but
I do believe that what I am doing, what I am constantly
working for, is what you really want from me in the long
run; and I have to take some things from you in order to
give you others. . . .

Well, maman, enough for tonight. Mille baisers. Je t'aime.
A bientot.

Ton enfant terrible qui travaille pour toi quand meme.

Uncle Harry was doing well and had moved to the Hudson Theatre. When would Miss LeG be auditioning for apprentices? When would she read the revised *Ilse?* Madeleine
and Marie vowed to wait at the back door after every performance of *Uncle Harry* in hopes of catching Miss LeG on her
way out.

Finally, one rainy afternoon, they got lucky. Miss LeG and
her companion, Marion Evensen, were standing at the stage
door after the matinee performance without an umbrella,

and Madeleine and Marie offered to run and get a taxi for them. Miss LeG, finding them both funny and delightful, gave them a ride, too, and Marie was finally able to introduce her to Madeleine in person. They were stunned at the address she gave—West Twelfth Street, which was just three blocks from their own apartment! It was fate. Miss LeG still didn't like the ending of *Ilse*, but since Madeleine had a comedy up her sleeve they quickly said they would send it, if Miss LeG would agree to read it. By the time they got to Twelfth Street, Madeleine and Marie felt as if they had really connected with Miss LeG and everything would be different now. Miss LeG told them to leave a copy of *'Phelia* at the stage door of the theater.

September 26, 1942
Mummy darlingest,

Guess who Marie and I rode down to her apartment on twelfth street from the Hudson in a taxi with? You may have three guesses. Right the first time. Miss Le Gallienne! And she was wonderful to us—so warm and friendly and un-cold and un-patronizing and marvellous! If I weren't going to see you so soon I don't think I could resist telephoning tonight. She still thinks the end of Ilse *is wrong, and she wants to have a talk and see if we can't put a finger on it, because she said she was very excited about the first two acts—and the end with Brand's suicide seems like putting something theatrical on a Tcheckov play. She treated me as a mature artist—and yet understanding that in many ways I'm still a child. There was no question about her wanting to read the new play. She wants to read anything I write. As you can probably see by this letter she made us delirious with joy. Oh, mother, if only she likes the new play. Both*

Pat and Cavada think it is infinitely better than Ilse but I don't know—I want to see what you think of it. I'll tell you about this afternoon more in detail when I see you—I've got to get it typed—the comedy I mean, not this afternoon!

Je t'aime a la folie—ton enfant heureuse.

PS Pat says to send you her love.

Madeleine typed the play and dropped it off for Miss LeG. A few weeks later, Marie called Miss LeG about 'Phelia. The director invited them over the very next day. When they got there Miss LeG said she hadn't had the chance to read it yet, and then talked about a book that she was writing, her overwhelming pile of correspondence, and how much she hated typing.

"I know how to type," Madeleine said. With those five words, Madeleine joined the inner circle: Miss LeG offered her a job answering her correspondence.

Those five words also marked the beginning of Madeleine's career and the end of her friendship with Marie.

Madeleine, circa 1943

Making a Living

Madeleine started going to the theater with Miss LeG on Tuesday and Thursday nights to go through her correspondence while Miss LeG was onstage, and then she would take the letters home and answer them. She and Marie also finally had the opportunity to audition for apprenticeships in the theater company for *Uncle Harry*. Marie eagerly prepared a very popular audition piece, the character Nina's monologue from Anton Chekhov's play *The Seagull*. Madeleine created an original monologue from Katherine Mansfield's autobiographical writings; she described the audition years later in a journal entry.

When I got out on the stage, trembling in every limb, to do my auditions, Miss Webster came up onto the stage and shook my hand, and said she was happy to meet me at last because she thought I was the most talented writer in the theater she knew anything about. The immensity of this didn't hit me til I got home I was so petrified about the audition. She just nodded after I finished and I couldn't tell what she thought. I was so frightened at the audition for Miss LeG two weeks later that I don't remember a thing about it! Later Miss LeG told me that both she and Miss Webster said to each other that if they hadn't known which was which they would have thought from the auditions that I was the actress and Marie the writer.

Marie and Madeleine were both selected as apprentices, but because of her job Madeleine was spending a lot more time with Miss LeG and was included in confidences and social activities that Marie was not. It surprised them both that Madeleine was the favorite, and Marie couldn't help feeling left out. Madeleine and Marie's friendship started to fray as Madeleine and Miss LeG's connection grew stronger.

Madeleine would later say that her relationship with Miss LeG wasn't quite friendship but more a case of hero worship, so much so that Mado was concerned about the influence this woman had over her daughter.

January 9, 1943
Mother darlingest,

Your letter this morning made me so happy after your last scoldy ones—and I'm still not sure what I'm being scolded about! But I'm glad you had the dream and that it made you feel happier—because, dearest, I do know that my contact with Miss Le Gallienne is good and will help me both as an artist and as a person. I had some wonderful talks with her while I was at the farm—and it was so good of her to let me just talk. She told me again how very much she believes in me as a playwright—and said that if I ever disappoint her she'll go shoot herself—not me!

I also asked her if she thought I should change my name. You know that I have been thinking of this for a long time. Do you remember once at the beach I was talking to Father about it and he suggested that I drop the "Camp" and call myself Madeleine L'Engle–and then he said something about maybe you mightn't like it because of Dannie [the original Madeleine L'Engle]–I'm a little confused about that part of it. Anyhow I've been thinking of doing that for a long time–remember, I signed most of my requests to summer theatres last spring "Madeleine L'Engle." Anyhow, when I said to Miss Le Gallienne, "Do you think I should change my name?" she said, "Yes, I do," and suggested that I drop the "Camp" saying that she thought names were terribly important (which I do, too) and that she thought I'd feel happier as "Madeleine L'Engle"–that she found it impossible to think of me as "Miss Camp" and didn't like to introduce me as that–it just didn't suit my personality at all. I've always thought it was a singularly ugly name . . . But anyhow, lamb, if it's all right with you, I think that I'll call myself Madeleine L'Engle.

It wasn't all right with her mother for Madeleine to drop her last name, not really, but Mado could only watch and worry from afar, and coax her daughter to send more letters and real news. Mado became more alarmed and concerned when Madeleine and Marie abruptly moved to an apartment on Twelfth Street with more roommates and no spare room for Mado. Mother and daughter argued, and Madeleine tried to explain that she, at twenty-four, was trying to be independent and that she needed to make her own decisions and even her own mistakes.

Still, for Mado, these moves felt like emotional abandonment. However, she continued to support Madeleine with a stipend and gifts of food and clothing. Marie didn't have that kind of family support, or the income Madeleine received from answering Miss LeG's letters, and she was dependent on Madeleine in ways that must have further strained their friendship.

When *Uncle Harry* closed in May 1943, the two young women needed to find summer-stock jobs until the theater company took the play on tour in the fall.

The Straight Wharf Theatre in Nantucket, where Madeleine and Marie had spent the previous summer, was in danger of closing down, so they worked together to make sure it survived. Marie and another friend from the company offered themselves as managers, which would help Marie in her ambition to be a producer and director. Madeleine would contribute two of her original plays—*'Phelia* and *The Christmas Tree*—and finally see them performed in front of live, paying audiences. Miss LeG and Margaret Webster were staunch advocates, and promised to come visit. Before Madeleine left, Miss Webster even arranged a preview of *The Christmas Tree* in New York and invited her friends to come see it.

However, it was a tough summer. *'Phelia* didn't go over well, and *The Christmas Tree* was too dark for the summer audiences.

One bright spot for Madeleine was an inquiry from an editor at Vanguard Press in response to a story Madeleine had published in a magazine called *New Threshold*.

In the fall of 1943, Madeleine and Marie were relieved to return to New York and go on tour with *Uncle Harry*. This meant living out of a suitcase, a different city every night, but Madeleine didn't mind. Being on tour brought the close theater community even closer. However, Marie was pulling away from Madeleine, and so Madeleine shared rooms with different female members of the company. Madeleine's part

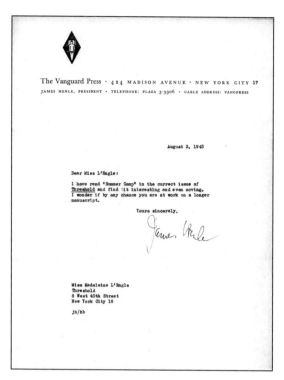

The Vanguard Press · 424 MADISON AVENUE · NEW YORK CITY 17
JAMES HENLE, PRESIDENT · TELEPHONE: PLAZA 3-3906 · CABLE ADDRESS: VANGPRESS

August 3, 1943

Dear Miss L'Engle:

I have read "Summer Camp" in the current issue of
Threshold and find it interesting and even moving.
I wonder if by any chance you are at work on a longer
manuscript.

Yours sincerely,

James Henle

Miss Madeleine L'Engle
Threshold
8 West 40th Street
New York City 18

jh/hb

in the play was small, just a few speaking lines. She was also writing a combination of a play and a novel. It was the story of Katherine, a pianist with a lonely childhood. Madeleine would steal time to write in her notebook between her scenes onstage and on trains going from one city to the next. Eventually this story became her first novel, *The Small Rain*.

Madeleine's first-draft notebook
for what would become her novel
The Small Rain

By the time the *Uncle Harry* company returned to New York, Marie had fallen out with Miss LeG and Madeleine. She left both the theater company and their apartment. It wasn't until more than two years later that Madeleine was able to write about that time.

The beginning of our association with Miss LeG was the end of Marie's and my friendship, though we didn't realize it then. Because right from the start I was the one with Miss LeG and Marie was not. I was the one whose talent she believed in, whose personality was interesting to her. I don't know who was more stunned at this, Marie or me. I had been completely accustomed to thinking of Marie as the superior one of the two of us, the beauty, the personality. I felt that people accepted me first because I was Marie's friend and second for myself.

Miss LeG and Margaret Webster's theater company followed up *Uncle Harry* with the production of a Chekhov play, *The Cherry Orchard*, on Broadway.

Still close to Miss LeG, Madeleine was an understudy and assistant stage manager. The company also needed someone to take care of Touché, a white poodle who was an integral part of the play, and knowing Madeleine was lonely and bruised from the breakup of her friendship with Marie, and a longtime dog lover, they asked that she take on that job, too. Madeleine was happy to do so. Touché, a truly professional performer, would lie completely still around Madeleine's neck like a fur stole in order to ride the subway back and forth to the theater undetected (since dogs were not allowed on the subway).

In June 1944, Vanguard Press offered Madeleine a one-hundred-dollar advance on *The Small Rain*. A hundred dollars

Madeleine and Touché,
circa 1945

was a small fortune in those days, and it allowed her to take the summer off to work full-time on a revision. All of her dreaming born of fiery determination was coming true—she was climbing the "alpine path" and writing her name on the scroll of fame.

Madeleine, circa 1944

Work and Love

Madeleine turned in her revision of *The Small Rain* in the fall of 1944 and joined the touring company of *The Cherry Orchard*. She was still in charge of Touché, and still an understudy. Since the Broadway run of *The Cherry Orchard* had been a box-office disappointment, the casting had been rethought and an actor named Hugh Franklin was now playing the role of Trofimov. He was tall and slim, and Madeleine was startled by his bright blue eyes. However, in her experience, men who got leading roles tended toward arrogance, so she assumed that she and Hugh were not going to be friends.

Hugh Hale Franklin, circa 1944

It turned out, though, that she was enchanted by him and he was equally enchanted by her. They soon found they had much in common. Both struggled with feeling like outsiders, both felt uncomfortable with the sometimes frantic social life of the theater crowd, and both loved Tchaikovsky—in particular his ballet *Swan Lake*—and they would use the music as a private signal between themselves.

But in many ways they were also opposites. Although Madeleine strove for emotional equilibrium, more often than not she was unable to maintain a stoic façade. Subject to moods and tempers, she was impulsive, sensitive, and demonstrative. Hugh kept a cool head during arguments and was much more reserved, private, and relaxed. Their life experiences were completely different, too. Hugh had grown up in Oklahoma with devout Baptist parents—no dancing, drinking, or cards—but he had studied at Northwestern University, north of Chicago, and had street smarts. Madeleine had a more cosmopolitan upbringing—with her childhood in New York, her early adolescence in France and Switzerland—and was going to be a published writer, but she was also naïve and gullible.

Sensing that Madeleine had no idea what life was like in places outside her own experience, Hugh teased her with stories about how the streets of Tulsa had only recently been paved, and how his mother only wore shoes when she went to church on Sundays. Madeleine's willingness to believe such things became a standing joke between them.

However, they had both chosen lives other than the ones expected of them (for Hugh's Baptist family, acting was quite scandalous), and both had grown up in families whose fortunes had changed drastically during the Great Depression following the stock market crash in 1929.

The theater company was watching their romance closely, perhaps too closely. Hugh, a very private person, was embarrassed by his fellow actors' scrutiny. He distanced himself from Madeleine and stopped sitting next to her on the train. Madeleine was hurt, but she didn't say anything. When Hugh gave her a pair of socks at Christmas, when the tour was over, instead of something more romantic, her hurt expanded into wounded pride, and she believed the relationship was over. As she had done with other disappointments, she tried to hide her pain from the world, channeling it instead into her writing and taking a break from Miss LeG and the theater company.

The Small Rain was published in January 1945. Reviews were good; most of the reviewers gave lots of encouragement to her as a young writer who had published her first novel.

"A warm, lovely story."
—Ruth Blodgett, *Book-of-the-Month Club News*

When Madeleine visited her mother in Jacksonville that winter, she was finally able to look at her relatives with pride, confident in the choices she had made.

Back in New York, Madeleine moved into a smaller apartment by herself on West Tenth Street, living alone for the first time.

In April 1945, Franklin Roosevelt died. Madeleine knew that Hugh was a great admirer of the president, and impulsively she called him. They spoke, but the conversation didn't lead anywhere, and she was again disappointed.

She threw herself back into her work, taking the play she had worked so hard on for Miss LeG, *Ilse*, and turning it into a novel with the same title (though now spelled as *Ilsa*). Set in Jacksonville, the story was a very uncomplimentary portrait of the South in the first half of the twentieth century, some of it based on Madeleine's own experiences with her extended family there. She submitted it to Vanguard, and it was accepted for publication.

That fall, shortly after the end of World War II, Hugh called. He was in town between shows—would she like to have dinner? Yes, she would. They saw a great deal of each other over the next few months, but they kept it private. Not even Mado, who visited for Madeleine's twenty-seventh birthday in November, was aware of how serious the two were.

Hugh proposed to Madeleine, with *Swan Lake* playing in the background, a few days after her birthday.

Very softly last night Hugh said the first two lines of that lovely poem of Conrad Aiken's.

[*Music I heard with you was more than music,*
And bread I broke with you was more than bread.]

We are going to be married.

> I would like to be able to write about this but somehow there aren't any words.

When her mother called to say she had arrived back home safely, Madeleine casually broke the news of her engagement. Hugh also telephoned his parents and then sent them a letter.

December 4, 1945
Dear Mother and Dad,

I should have written all this before telephoning you so it wouldn't have been such a great shock, but I must say it sounded like less of a shock to you than I thought it would. But I wanted you to know as soon as possible and I also wanted you to mail the ring right away so Madeleine could have it by Sunday. Funny about the ring—when I told her that you had a ring, Mother, that you had always said would be mine when I found the right girl, she said "Well, I want an old-fashioned one with a diamond held up on prongs" and I told her that was exactly what this one was as I remembered it.

I can assure you you'll love Madeleine as much as I do. She's not a Miss America by any means but she has more personality than any Miss America ever had. If you have found a copy of The Small Rain *you'll see a picture of her on the cover. She's quite tall—I think almost 5'9" and has always been self conscious of it—she needn't be now. She's always worn flat heels but is now wearing high ones! She's not so much blond as light haired, has a high forehead which she camouflages with bangs. Her eyesight is not good but she hates to wear her glasses, consequently can't see very well. I think that's why she picked me.*

Hugh was about to go on tour with *A Joyous Season*, and Madeleine auditioned for an understudy part. "Don't give it to her on my account," Hugh told the producer. Madeleine, capable of getting the job on her own merits, was hired.

Hugh and Madeleine, January 26, 1946, at Saint Chrysostom's Church in Chicago

Their engagement was brief, only eight weeks, and they married on January 26, 1946, in Chicago.

No family were able to come on such short notice, but a friend from the company stood up for them in church. When the theater tour was over, Hugh moved in with Madeleine in the apartment on West Tenth Street.

Madeleine and Hugh, circa 1946

Marriage and Children

*I*t was a happy time for the newlyweds. The war was over, and *Ilsa* was published in March to solid reviews. Since she was already published and known professionally as Madeleine L'Engle, Madeleine continued to use that name, though she was also known by her married name, Madeleine Franklin, in her personal life.

Hugh's star, too, seemed to be on the rise, with work plentiful and rewarding.

Yet the couple had a sense of dissatisfaction and restlessness. What had thrilled Madeleine when she was fresh out of college was different from what she wanted as a married woman whose career as a novelist— instead of a playwright—was taking off. She was working on

"Miss L'Engle has the happy gift of never being obvious. She writes with subtlety and in realizing her characters, she suggests rather than explains. She has created in Ilsa a memorable figure and a challenge to the imagination." —Polly Goodwin, *The Chicago Tribune*

several novels, including *And Both Were Young*, with a teenage protagonist, Flip, inspired by her days at boarding school. And although she still had jobs in the theater, she did not feel as attached to it as she once had—she hadn't been involved with Miss LeG and Margaret Webster's theater company for some months. Things that had brought Madeleine and Hugh together—feelings of being out of place in the social life of the theater—remained, and they began to think about making a change.

> More and more we want to get out of the city, away from artificiality. The longer we work in the theatre the more we realize it is the place we want to work and the more we realize that it is essential for us to make many friends out of the theatre. We have got to the point where this company bores us to hysteria. Although alone they are all interesting, nice people, when they are together they seem to set up a reaction, to represent everything superficial and artificial. And after an evening of being clever, always with a little edge of smirk to the cleverness, of brilliant surface conversation, we come out feeling wasted and soiled. People ought to stay apart if that is what happens when they get together.

Madeleine loved New York City, with its vibrancy, its color. She could be anonymous and solitary when she wanted to be, yet there were plenty of opportunities for connection and culture when she needed them. Hugh was less happy with the city—its noise, its dirt, and their small quarters—but it was where the work was. They dreamed of having six children, of creating a family life quite different from Madeleine's solitary upbringing. She wanted dogs and cats, too—she'd always loved them but had never had any of her own, not counting Touché.

Madeleine and Hugh had friends who had given up on the theater and moved to northwestern Connecticut, and Madeleine had fond memories of spending summers at Camp Huckleberry in that same area. When Madeleine became pregnant in late 1946, they bought an old, rambling farmhouse in Goshen, Connecticut, near their friends, so they could spend weekends and summers in the country. They called it Crosswicks, the same name as Madeleine's father's childhood hometown in New Jersey.

Crosswicks, circa 1954

Soon enough, the baby came due. Madeleine had a difficult labor and delivery, and then she had to be rushed back to the hospital after a month because of complications. It was only after that scare was over that she was able to enjoy her newborn daughter, Josephine, and get used to the rhythms of motherhood, which didn't include much writing.

Madeleine and Josephine, circa 1948

Hugh traveled a great deal—he was on tour with another play—so Madeleine and Josephine were without him for much of the time that first year, but Mrs. O, Madeleine's staunch supporter, was a frequent visitor at their apartment. Madeleine and Josephine also visited Mado and other relatives in Jacksonville.

Those visits to Jacksonville were tense because Madeleine's extended family thought her marriage had been hasty and a little scandalous. They also felt Madeleine had aired some family "dirty laundry" in *Ilsa*. Her cousins snubbed her, and her mother was distraught and embarrassed. Madeleine was deeply wounded and hurt by this: she didn't understand how or why her family couldn't simply be proud of her success, and not offended by the family descriptions that hit too close to home.

When one tour ended and another began for Hugh in the summer of 1947, they decided that Madeleine and the baby should spend an extended period at Crosswicks. She was writing, but her new novel wasn't going well. She put it aside when Beatrice Creighton, an editor at the publisher Lothrop, Lee & Shepard who had been considering *And Both Were Young*, asked for some changes to the manuscript so it could be published as a "juvenile book." This was something Madeleine had never thought of or tried before.

It has been a full summer and, on the whole, a good one. If Creighton is pleased with my book I shall be happy and if she is not I shall be miserable. The entire summer is going to be colored in my mind by her reaction to it. I know that is foolish and perhaps it is wrong, but it is the truth of the matter and there is nothing I can do about it. As I look back on this summer it will be the fate of Flip that will determine color.

The colors were glorious for Madeleine, as *And Both Were Young* was accepted for publication. It came out in 1949.

"A boarding school story for girls is sure of popularity. Madeleine L'Engle has chosen Geneva for the scene of her unusually good tale of a lovely American girl in an international school . . . The author, former secretary to Eva Le Gallienne, has had personal experience in boarding schools."
—*Horn Book*

Madeleine then started work on *Camilla Dickinson*, a coming-of-age novel set in her beloved New York City. She returned to her favorite themes of adolescence and those moments when you realize that your parents aren't perfect, that they have separate lives, and that you are the one responsible for your own happiness. This imaginative return to the New York of her childhood made her ponder her process.

At 31 I am still beset with all the passions, depressions, exultations of adolescence. Some of adolescence I don't want to lose—the sudden awareness of discovery—discovery of all kinds of things, books, pictures, music, sunsets, stars, common trees, night, food, drink, people...But the other part, the unreasonable moods, glooms, tortures, self-doubts, the unwillingness to grow up: those I wish I could lose. It's a difficult balance to strike. To be [a] writer, the kind of writer I want to be, I must keep certain qualities of adolescence, but it must be passion that is productive; out of the gloom must come light. And above all I must not use it as an excuse to remain childish. I myself must mature if I can hope to have my writing become mature.

I have asked myself frequently of late why writing is so desperately important to me. Or, more simply: why do I write?

And the only really honest answer I can give is: "I have to."

But why I have to I can't truly say. It is just a necessary function to me like breathing and eating and eliminating. And is one of my greatest joys. And one of my greatest agonies.

And what do I want to do with my writing? Again that's a question I find difficult to answer to myself. I can feel what I want to do, but I can't put it in words that satisfy myself. I don't believe in propaganda writing as a form of art but I would like my books to make their readers want to be more than they are, to reach higher. I want to make them—the readers—aware of the

122

wonderfully exciting and unlimited possibilities of man. Perhaps I am a romantic because I don't want to make them disappointed in their surroundings but with themselves. And not too much of that, really. What I want them to feel is: look! How wonderful I can be if I only will and I will! How wonderful everyone can be!

And as I look back on my finished books I know I have not done this. Perhaps because it is something I need to feel more often myself.

But I must write. I must "be a writer" in the fullest sense of the word. I must someday begin to approach more nearly what I'm striving for.

And now I sound 16 again. Perhaps talking about being mature always sounds immature.

In the fall of 1951, Madeleine and Hugh decided to live full-time at Crosswicks. Madeleine was pregnant again. They were still hoping for lots more children and thought it would be easier to raise them in the country. Hugh would use Crosswicks as a home base while he pursued acting jobs, and Madeleine, of course, could write anywhere.

Camilla Dickinson had been accepted for publication. Madeleine's publisher also wrote to her about some praise she'd received of a different sort—*Pageant* magazine had named her one of the ten most beautiful female authors of 1951.

Hugh's career as an actor hadn't become more predictable or stable. He would work for a few grueling months on tour and then just wait, wait, wait for a call for the next job.

The theatre is the goddamnest lousiest most heartbreaking profession. Sometimes I think I can't stand it for Hugh, the gaps in between jobs, the appointments and then the waiting. And the

"Ms. L'Engle's Camilla has more innate strength and stability than Salinger's Holden Caulfield."
—Harrison Smith, *Saturday Review*

telephone. The telephone has become a horrible personality dominating the room. Waiting for it to ring for a job or even an appointment. And then waiting to see if you get the job. Sometimes it seems to me that Jo and I are millstones around his neck as far as the theater is concerned. With the amount of television he's done this year he could have done very well and even saved something. As it is we just barely managed. Having a child invariably raises your standard of living—and we have the house, too—and all that can't help but weigh heavily on his mind.

With the publication of *Camilla Dickinson* shortly after their move, though, Madeleine herself was feeling secure in her identity as a writer.

She was also confident that village life would suit her and her writing. She and Hugh joined the local Congregational Church, where Madeleine was the choir director and occasional Sunday school teacher. She was determined to be part of the community, and was very happy that both the children she taught and the parents at the church enjoyed her.

Perhaps one reason this makes me so happy, is so important to me, is that it has taken me so long to get on with people, to become outgoing instead of in going. And since, until I was about 14, I wasn't able to get on with other children, it pleases me to have children like me now.

She was solidifying her writing philosophy, too, and understanding the anguish she had experienced as a child at the opera. For her as a writer, stories were meant to transform both the reader and the main character—she did not want them to end in tragedy.

I've felt for some time now (a definite development from my collegiate point of view) that the end of a work of fiction should be positive, that no matter how tragic or sordid the events the reader should be left at the end with a feeling of elevation.

Madeleine also admitted that moving to rural Connecticut was an escape of sorts. Having been a child in Europe as the shadow of World War II was lengthening, Madeleine had long feared war. Now, as a mother, she worried about a new type of war dominating the news of the day: a cold war between two superpowers armed with nuclear weapons.

Each morning while Jo and I are eating breakfast there is a half hour news broadcast from eight to eight thirty. I try to listen to it and yet to keep chattering to Jo so that she won't have to hear most of it, because even if she can't understand the words she can sense the fear and tension behind it. And I think rather ashamedly that one reason I am glad we are here this winter instead of in New York (though it is not the reason) is a kind of escapism. I listen to the news but it does not seem as close here as it does in New York, even when it's on the same programs we listened to most there, WNYC or WQXR. And in this lulled sense of false security I no longer have the nightmares about atom bombs or the panic for the safety of my children. I know this is being like an ostrich with its head in the sand. Goshen, given the right circumstances, could easily become a little hell of its own . . . And though I might feel that I was on the side of the angels that wouldn't change the terror of the powers of darkness.

Madeleine and Hugh's second child, Bion, named after Madeleine's grandfather, was born in March 1952.

Madeleine and Bion, 1952

Madeleine again had problems giving birth, and she and Hugh received the news that they couldn't have any more children. It was a devastating blow to them both.

It was around this time that Hugh also made the decision to leave the theater and try something else. What that something else would be, he didn't know; he only knew that if he wasn't going to be a successful actor, he was running out of time to start a new career, and his young family needed a more stable income.

Hugh took jobs at a factory and a radio station before buying the local general store in Goshen. He ran the store, and Madeleine worked there part-time.

She was also a housewife and mother, but she wasn't like the other mothers in her community. She was the only one in town who was trying to do something else in addition to the hard and necessary work of keeping house and home and, in some cases, farm.

Goshen general store

Madeleine at the store, circa 1958

It was lonely being different. She began to understand how her father's isolation as an artist had affected him. She also began to realize that her mother had never been able to understand that about her father, and she worried that perhaps Hugh might not be able to understand that about her either.

After a couple of years, village life began to wear. Madeleine and Hugh had their artist, actor, and writer friends visit from New York on the weekends, and some of their friends in Goshen had started a community theater company called the Goshen Players, which Madeleine joined. Hugh was more reluctant to keep a toe in the theater. It was painful and frustrating to do as a hobby what he had planned on doing as a career.

Madeleine carved out time to write, but it was always at the kitchen table and often interrupted. She did maintain her discipline of practicing the piano for half an hour every day, which sometimes was the only thing in her routine keeping her tied to her creative life. She continued to use her journal to record ideas for future work.

> 24-8-53
>
> 'A Tesseract is a concept, arrived at by the following reasoning: here we have a one dimensional line a. From such lines form a two-dimensional square, a^2, which is bounded by four lines and has four vertices (corners). Four such squares form the three dimensional cube, a^3, which is bounded by six squares, has twelve edges and four vertices. The four-dimensional cube, called Hypercube or Tesseract, would be mathematically described as a^4 and we can state that it should be bounded by 8 cubes, have 16 vertices, 24 faces, and 32 edges. But since it is supposed to be 4 dimensional we obviously can't make one.

October 4, 1953

A Tesseract is a concept, arrived at by the following reasoning: here we have a one dimensional line a. Four such lines form a two-dimensional square a^2, which is bounded by four lines and has four vertices (corners). Four such squares form the three dimensional cube, a^3, which is bounded by six squares, has twelve edges and four vertices. The four dimensional cube, called Hypercube or Tesseract, would be mathematically described as a^4 and we can state that it should be bounded by 8 cubes, have 16 vertices, 24 faces, and 32 edges. But since it is supposed to be 4 dimensional we obviously can't make one.

Perhaps one can reconcile the contradiction between predestination and free will by thinking of the sonnet: within the strict boundaries of the form there is great freedom.

During this time she had managed to complete two new novels, *Rachel* and *A Winter's Love*, but they were rejected in quick succession.

Let us face a few facts.

I worked hard on "Rachel" but I never saw either the book or my major characters clearly. I was bitterly disappointed [by] its failure. I was still struggling with rebellion against living in the country. I wanted New York and the life of New York so abominably that it was like a sickness. My own personal individual life was utterly confused and filled with conflicts. I expected for some reason that this new book—the Emily book—would fall into my lap without any real effort on my part. This never happens . . .

> Let me realize that I cannot accomplish a full day's work in a couple of tired hours a night.
>
> Let me realize that I cannot write a valid book without at least as much labour as it takes to produce a child.

It was the 1950s, well into the Cold War, and anticommunism was captivating the nation. The arms race between the United States and the Soviet Union had created a great deal of fear. Senator Joseph McCarthy was in charge of investigating "un-American activities" in the United States, and his tactics stirred up such fear that some people began thinking of each other as "spies." McCarthy held a series of investigations and hearings, some secret, some televised, accusing individual scientists and artists of having ties to the Communist Party and the Soviet Union. There was even a Hollywood blacklist containing the names of anyone even suspected of sympathizing with communism. Those on the list were no longer hired for work.

Madeleine opposed ideological fervor in any of its forms; she saw in McCarthyism a danger as grave as many saw in communism.

> During McCarthy's investigation of [J. Robert] Oppenheimer one of the charges against the scientist was that he had delayed in the production of the H Bomb. Both McCarthy and the News stated that the only possible reason Oppenheimer could have had for holding back on the H Bomb was the subversive one of withholding aid from the United States and giving it to Russia. Not one mention of Oppenheimer's conscience made. Not once was it suggested that perhaps morally he hesitated to make possible a weapon that could destroy our world entirely, that could cause

> the ghastly murders of billions of people . . . If anybody is blinding us to the fact that there are communists; and that they are a menace, it is McCarthy. Let us try, in opposing him, not to fall into the pattern he has set. It is more than a pattern; it is a trap.

The McCarthy hearings consumed and terrified her even more than the threat of war did. The false promises of security through purity of thought and ideology and McCarthy's methods of investigation, intimidation, and guilt by association weighed on her mind, and she began to explore a creative response.

She got a new agent, Theron Raines, to represent her work to publishers. Theron was optimistic and encouraging, and agreed to take on *Rachel* and *A Winter's Love*. Even if she knew she would never stop writing, that it was as essential to her as breathing, Madeleine also cared desperately about being successful and acknowledged.

> Each day I feel a little more desperate. Another part of it is that my faith in myself as a writer is what makes life in Goshen bearable. It's nothing to do with or against Goshen. But basically I'm a big city person, and though I know we're better off here than in New York I'll never, no matter how wildly I succeed on the outside, be anything but a misfit on the inside. But all right—I don't mind the lack of people I can talk to in my own language, the hours spent at the store, having to snatch my writing hours at night when I am tired, as long as I have faith in myself as a writer. Without that everything dissolves into resentment and hate, hate for the store, the lack of culture, of intellectual stimulation, even of simple appreciation for music or pictures or books—hate and resentment and a feeling of waste. If Theron doesn't like this

book there is no need for me to lose faith in myself and my work, but it's been too long since anything I've written has been considered acceptable; I'm in desperate need now of encouragement, not discouragement.

And the only reason I'm writing all this, or anything I write in these journals at all, is that it may be useful to me in a book someday. When I first started writing journals it was with the usual idea for publication; now I know that outside of fiction what I write is inhibited and dull, but the gem of life is there to remind me of some only barely indicated emotion so that I will have it when I need it.

When she developed severe stomach pain, Madeleine and her doctor both wondered if it was psychosomatic, due to her worry over her writing. But the pain worsened; in addition, she had a flare-up of iritis, for which she spent nearly three weeks in the hospital in the fall of 1955. The best medical advice was "rest," which she tried. She also tried to not worry so much about her writing.

Finally, in 1957, *A Winter's Love* was accepted and published.

"A village in the French Alps serves as an appropriate setting for this novel of a marriage that nearly fails." —*The Tribune*, South Bend, Indiana

Sadly, Madeleine's happiness at succeeding with a new book was cut short. She and Hugh had two friends, Liz Dewing and Arthur Richmond, who had spent several summer vacations with them in Connecticut. Liz and Arthur died suddenly, just a few months apart, leaving behind their daughter, Maria. At seven years old, a devastated Maria came to live at Crosswicks, joining nine-year-old Josephine and four-year-old Bion.

Bion, Mado, Maria, and Josephine, with dogs Gardie and Oliver, circa 1959

Now that her household numbered five, Madeleine, more than ever, needed to find space and time to write. She and Hugh built an office for her over the garage in 1958.

Madeleine in "The Tower," her Crosswicks office, circa 1959

A *Winter's Love* didn't sell as well as Madeleine had hoped, and *Rachel*, which she had revised as many as six times over the years, was making the rounds without much interest. Madeleine turned back to where she'd had success: writing about younger protagonists, as she'd done in *And Both Were Young*. She started to work on *Meet the Austins*, which began as a series of vignettes about a family living in a New England village.

The book about the Austins found a publisher who wanted significant changes: more plot, something with a recognizable crisis and resolution. The novel had been inspired by Madeleine's own family life, and since her family was in the process of integrating Maria into the household, the central drama became the arrival of a newly orphaned girl named Maggy. This fictionalization proved to be hurtful to Madeleine's own children while they were growing up, something Madeleine never fully understood.

Madeleine was happy to be writing well again, and around this time Hugh realized he would never be happy if he wasn't acting. Running the general store was no longer a challenge for him, and he was restless. But the thought of returning to acting was daunting—he had been out of the game so long. Also, how would it be possible to raise a family on such an unstable income? Although *Meet the Austins* had found a publisher, the couple was under no illusions that Madeleine's income as a writer could support the family if Hugh's return to the theater failed. Yet Madeleine had come to understand that failure might be making her more of a writer than success had done—because if you fail, and then keep going no matter what, that is what makes you a writer. It almost doesn't have anything to do with publishing. So Madeleine supported Hugh wholeheartedly in his decision— she knew she wasn't fully alive unless she was doing the work she loved, and she wanted the same for her husband. Still, it was not an easy decision.

Now that the decision is made, I'm scared.

There is a seductive safety in the store...I'm scared stiff about a return to the theater! All the things that made Hugh miserable before are still there. What do we do about the children and their education? We can't afford private schools in New York. How long can we keep them in school here and manage on a commuting basis? What do we do between jobs? When will the first job come? What about the long periods when we will have to be separated? They were bad before; they will be harder now. Will we be able to manage financially?

Madeleine, circa 1961

Making the Leap

Madeleine and Hugh sold the store, and Hugh started spending more time in New York City looking for acting jobs. He was away from the family and Goshen for long stretches of time, but he wasn't able to find work. By the end of the spring of 1959, the couple decided to take a two-month cross-country camping trip before Hugh started to look for work again. They piled into the family station wagon and set off for California, visiting Hugh's relatives in Oklahoma and stopping at some of the country's most beautiful national parks along the way. They slept in a tent, did their cooking over a fire, and rose and slept with the sun.

Preparing for the family camping trip, 1959

It was while driving across the country, through varied and new landscapes, without much thought of what lay ahead, that Madeleine's imagination began connecting the dots between sonnets and tesseracts, security and risk, love and action.

Day by day living on this trip, never planning ahead, has been good for me in that it has made it more possible to face complete uncertainty and insecurity of the future. Newspapers and radio have kept world tensions with us, but even they have seemed further away than they do at home.

As we neared the New Mexico Border we went into a Ute Indian reservation, and suddenly the country changed entirely. It changed so completely that we might have been in another planet. Everyplace else we've been so far has been a little familiar to me, at least a little like someplace else I've seen; but this was like [artist] Chesley Bonestell's pictures of alien worlds. Dry brown land with sparse, dull green vegetation. High mountainous cliffs with flat tops and eroded sides. And strange fairy tale rock formations appearing out of nowhere.

Painted Desert, Arizona. The first real beauty so far in Arizona. Red, lava-like cones and pyramids stretching out to the horizon on yellow desert. Purple and blue shadows. Again like the surface of another planet.

Madeleine later recalled that the characters of Mrs Whatsit, Mrs Who, and Mrs Which popped into her head while driving through the Painted Desert in Arizona.

When they got back from their trip, Madeleine and the children got ready for the beginning of the school year in Connecticut, and Hugh at last found a theater job: he would play the father, Otto, in a production of *The Diary of Anne Frank* at a summer theater in Massachusetts.

Madeleine and the children joined him in New York in February of 1960. By that time, Madeleine had written the first draft for what would eventually be called *A Wrinkle in Time*. Her working title was *Mrs Whatsit, Mrs Who, and Mrs Which*. Although Madeleine hadn't studied hard at Le Châtelard, she did retain the school's use of British grammar, punctuation, and spelling rules. She thought the absence of the period after *Mrs*, a Britishism, added to her characters' otherworldliness.

Madeleine, circa 1965

After *Anne Frank*, Hugh was cast in a production of Gore Vidal's *The Best Man*, which was doing a test run in a theater close to Lincoln Center before heading to Broadway, so the family was living in a hotel near there. Friends had encouraged them to look for a house in the suburbs outside the city, but they knew that Madeleine would feel as isolated as she had in Connecticut and that Hugh would have a long commute. They decided to find an apartment in Manhattan.

While Hugh was in rehearsals, Madeleine and the children concentrated their efforts on those parts of the city she knew best: Greenwich Village and the Upper East Side, but everything they saw was either too expensive or too small. Then Josephine saw an ad in the newspaper for a six-room apartment on the Upper West Side. At first Madeleine didn't want to go look—she didn't know much about the neighborhood, and she was sure that something that size would be beyond their budget. But Josephine insisted on trudging all the way up to 105th Street and Broadway, and they found that the apartment was indeed affordable and the neighborhood was a jumble of different kinds of people, something that Madeleine had loved about Greenwich Village.

Soon the children were settled in a school not far from the apartment, and Madeleine worked on revising *Mrs Whatsit, Mrs Who, and Mrs Which.* She was frustrated that the publisher who had taken *Meet the Austins* still hadn't given her any editorial notes or a publication date.

Monday I finished typing Mrs Whatsit and gave it into Theron. So there is that awful feeling of being through with one book and not started on another. And the feeling of terror.

142

Hugh's play was a success, which meant they could be a little less anxious about money. It also meant a new routine for the two of them. Madeleine stayed up late in order to have some time with him after he got home from work, and they didn't go to bed before two in the morning. She was also up early with the children, getting them ready for school. That, and the worry over *Mrs Whatsit, Mrs Who, and Mrs Which* making the rounds with publishers brought a flare-up of her stomach trouble. Mrs. O came to help, and on her suggestion the household made an adjustment: the children, led by Josephine, who was now thirteen, got themselves breakfasted and off to school in the mornings by themselves. Madeleine and Hugh still had time together, and Madeleine got the sleep she needed. If the children missed their parents in the morning, they had their company and attention in the evenings, when eating dinner around the family table before Hugh went to the theater was a hard-and-fast rule.

But the rejections for *Mrs Whatsit* started to come, including from Madeleine's editor at Vanguard Press, Evelyn Shrifte.

Evelyn turned down *Mrs Whatsit* while I was there, turned it down with one hand while saying that she loved it, but didn't quite dare do it, as it isn't really classifiable. I know it isn't really classifiable, and am wondering if I'll have to go through the usual hell with this that I seem to go through with everything I write. But this book I'm sure of, as I wasn't of *A Winter's Love*, or even of the *Austins*. I know *Mrs Whatsit* is a good book, and if I've ever written a book that says what I feel about God and the universe, this is it. This is my psalm of praise to life, my stand for life against death.

After a second rejection, she wrote in her journal:

In a book I'm reading about Fitzgerald, there is a sentence about "second-rate writers who pass themselves off as geniuses." But how does anybody know? A writer is far too tied up in his work, if he is really a writer, to know whether it is second rate or a work of genius. And how many writers who have been considered second rate, and yet who have persisted in believing in themselves, have been discovered and hailed as geniuses years after their deaths; or writers who have been highly acclaimed during their lives have been forgotten forever shortly after? Or writers who are perhaps true geniuses who have never been discovered at all?

Perhaps all this is true if someone just decides at the age of twenty or thirty or fourty, oh, I think I'll try to write. But what about those of us who are stuck with it? Does it really matter if we are geniuses or if we are second rate? It is something that is as much a part of us as the colour of our hair.

After a third, this:

I hate to have to tell mother because it will just make her un-happy. She went through it with father and now with me. But father had had a lot more success, he'd been a lot more important.

In the fall of 1960, while she was in limbo with *Mrs Whatsit, Mrs Who, and Mrs Which* and *Meet the Austins* still hadn't come out, Madeleine decided to go back to school and take classes at Columbia University, not far from where the family lived.

I'm going back to school. Taking a course at Columbia with three credits towards an M.A. I'm really very pleased and excited. It doesn't start for a couple of weeks—a course on advanced novel writing by Caroline Gordon. I know her work and respect it, and hope that the course will give me the stimulation and excitement and more of a legitimate reason for keeping at the typewriter. The children will understand it a little more if I say, "I have to do my homework, too."

She enjoyed some friendships, playing piano duets with one new friend and reconnecting with old theater friends for dinners. She volunteered at the children's school, directing the annual Christmas pageant; kept working on *Rachel*; and, at the suggestion of her old friend Herbert Berghof, started a play adaptation of the book *The Love Letters of a Portuguese Nun*, which had scandalized Europe in the late seventeenth century.

But the *Mrs Whatsit, Mrs Who, and Mrs Which* rejections kept coming.

Each rejection, no matter how philosophically expected, is a wound. Perhaps the thing about it that bothers me the most is that the editor, in returning it to Theron, said that he felt that it should be cut at least in half, and that he thought Theron should do this before sending it to another publisher. And Theron was all for talking to him on Monday and seeing if he'd be interested in it, if I cut it in half. I'm willing to rewrite, to rewrite extensively, to cut as much as necessary; but I am not willing to mutilate, to destroy the essence of the book. I told Theron to go ahead and talk to him if he was determined to, but that this was how I felt. And I added that one has to keep some integrity. I won't destroy my book for money for some editor who completely misses the point, which this one obviously did.

One of the reasons she felt so strongly about not making those changes to the manuscript, changes she thought violated the book's heart, was that she had gone against her similar instincts with *Meet the Austins*, and it bothered her. When she heard in October that the *Austins* jacket was finalized and the book would be released in November, she was anxious instead of being excited. Then came the first review, calling it "a convincing and attractive picture of a family faced with real and important issues."

This clipping [of the review] came on Thursday, and was a relief rather than a joy. Things have gone badly with my writing for so long that I can hardly believe that it is possible that something may go right: and it is the basic inner faith that eventually it will that keeps me going.

Then, just before Christmas, Madeleine received word from Theron that another publisher who had had *Mrs Whatsit, Mrs Who, and Mrs Which* for a long time had also decided to pass. Once more, she was devastated. Hugh, too, was having some professional disappointments. While the run of *The Best Man* was continuing, he had only a minor part and wanted to try something else, something with more challenge and visibility, but he was not getting callbacks.

Meet the Austins

By MADELEINE L'ENGLE

Author of the 1963 Newbery Medal Winner

"A convincing and attractive picture of a family faced with real and important issues." —*V. Kirkus Bulletin*

I have told Theron to bring me back *Mrs Whatsit*, to bring me back *Rachel*. The entire last third of *Rachel* is wrong, and I want to look at *Mrs Whatsit* again before he sends it anywhere else. I want to make Meg's return to Camazotz for Charles Wallace more motivated.

It's not clear, however, that she had a chance to make any changes to *Mrs Whatsit* before she had a call from John Farrar, of the publishing company Farrar, Straus and Giroux.

I had a talk with John Farrar this afternoon which was also hopeful. He is not only a good friend of Hester Stover's, he's a good publisher, and Hester talked to him about me, and he knew and remembered *The Small Rain* and looked through three other of my books and I'm to come talk to him. And as Hugh says, this is much more the way things get done than when a manuscript is sent in cold by an agent. He knows and likes Theron, too. And then I told him that *Mrs Whatsit* was difficult to classify, but that if I had to compare it to anything it would be one of C. S. Lewis' parables, he said that C. S. Lewis was right up his alley. So he is to make an appointment (he called me from home) and I'm to come in and talk to him and someone else in the office about it. Oh, I can't help hoping, I can't help hoping.

Madeleine brought Farrar the manuscript on January 16. The following day, she was already anxious that she hadn't heard from him, even though she must have known that was an unrealistic expectation. But, on January 18, she heard from Theron.

Mr. Farrar likes *Mrs Whatsit*, [and] the juvenile man there likes it, but they're a little afraid of it and are going to give it to an outside reader to report on. So. My first reaction, I'm afraid, was frustrated rage. I'd so hoped that they'd like it, say so, and buy it. But at least I still have hope. And I will just have to wait and see. If there is karma, mine is certainly patience.

Almost two more weeks passed before Madeleine's patience had its reward.

Happiness is as numbing as unhappiness. Bion came into our room this morning (there's a teacher's conference so no school) and said, "Mommie, Theron says I'm to wake you up. He wants to speak to you. It must be very important." Farrar is taking *Mrs Whatsit*.

Madeleine, Charlotte, and Léna, circa 1970

Epilogue

*I*t was supposed to be a quiet book. John Farrar loved it and was willing to publish it, but he thought that the audience would be very narrow—it was a risk. If science fiction in the late 1950s and early 1960s was published primarily with male readers in mind, how would people respond to a fault-ridden female protagonist who has to become her own hero? And weren't the book's concepts about space and time, and good and evil, over children's heads? But he was willing to gamble on it because he believed in Madeleine as a writer, and he wagered that if *A Wrinkle in Time* didn't do well, her next book would.

The response, however, ended up being overwhelming, as both children and adults were able to see themselves in the main character, Meg Murry, and were swept up in the great adventure. Teachers and librarians championed *A Wrinkle in Time*, and because of its success, Madeleine was able to spend her time from then on lecturing, teaching, and writing, without the guilt she'd felt during the years in Connecticut because she was neither successful in the ways she wanted to be as a writer nor accomplished in the domestic virtues that were so lauded in the 1950s.

Madeleine and Newbery committee chair Ruth Gagliardo

During the 1960s, she wrote books and traveled and saw her three children safely out of the nest. Eventually, she became a grandmother.

We knew her as GrandMadeleine, or Gran, and were very close: summers and Christmases loom large in our own memories, and after our grandfather Hugh (we called him "Gum," short for Grumpy Old Grandpa, which he tried to teach us to say) died, we lived with her when we were both in college in New York. Charlotte stayed on with her in the apartment through graduate school.

She always felt like "one of us" and always seemed to be whatever age we were, a comrade and fellow traveler who also nurtured and supported us. She was the woman who sang at the top of her lungs, who played Ping-Pong with gusto, and

who had us all read Shakespeare aloud, cuddled up in her four-poster bed. She was the lonely girl who craved connection and who, as an adult, recognized and responded to that need in others. She was the woman who shared her spontaneity and grace by showing us the stars, whether outside at a special star-watching rock near Crosswicks or at the planetarium, or even by pointing out our own inner light.

As young children, we were invited into the heart of her writing life. At Crosswicks, the family called her writing room above the garage "the Tower," short for "Madeleine's Ivory Tower," a wry reference to scholarly seclusion and privilege. It was off-limits to everyone else except by special invitation, though we, her granddaughters, were always welcome, much to the shock of the rest of the family, who had been trained to give it a wide berth. The Tower was lined with bookcases filled with fiction, nonfiction, large art books, mass-market paperbacks, and standard as well as more esoteric reference books. Various editions of her own books were there, too, and best of all to us: shelves and shelves of manuscript boxes with handwritten titles we didn't recognize, three-ring binders with the mysterious word *mélanges* on the spine, and books of different sizes and shapes and bindings, which we knew were her journals. Her whole history as a writer was laid before our eyes.

She had a big desk that had belonged to her father nestled next to a huge window overlooking Mohawk Mountain. The desk was always a mess of papers, pens, small boxes, and figurines, including a Buddha, a giraffe, and various religious icons. Her typewriter was on a special smaller table to the side. A dog would always be by her feet.

We would sprawl on the daybed opposite the desk, and she let us read whatever we wanted. We understood that the journals were private, so we never ventured into those sacred texts. *Mélanges*, we eventually learned, is French for "mixture," and those notebooks were filled with lectures and old college papers. Some of her manuscripts held no fascination for us once we read the first few pages: they were about adults, and we were not interested in those stories. But there was *Brigitta*, set in a Swiss boarding school with a fearless protagonist who led the other girls in various acts of independence, and *The Joys of Love*, about a young actor's first job at a summer theater by the sea.

There was also an electronic piano in the Tower, and Gran would occasionally get up from her typewriter and do finger exercises—scales and arpeggios—or attempt a complicated composition like Bach's Toccata in C Minor. She said it helped "clear the cobwebs out." She said she never minded practicing the piano when she was younger (that made us skeptical: we hated practicing!), and that in fact, that, too, had helped her become a writer.

"How?" we asked.

"Discipline. I saw how if my mother didn't practice every day, her playing suffered. It's the same for a writer. You have to practice every day. I also saw how she could go to the piano in a bad mood and usually come away an hour later in a much better frame of mind. I was terribly disorganized and undisciplined in every other way, but I developed enormous discipline for writing, because it was the only thing that ever made me happy when I was younger."

As we grew older, our conversations grew deeper, particularly on summer nights as teenagers when we hiked out to the star-watching rock to wonder at the sky. One night, when one of us was feeling particularly wretched about a falling-out with friends, we went to the rock. She told us a story about a time during her theater days when she had been feeling particularly wretched, too, and confided that her mentor, the great actress Eva Le Gallienne, had told her a secret.

"What was that?" we asked.

"Miss LeG wore a locket around her neck. The secret was that in the locket, instead of a picture, was a note that said: *Everyone is lonely.*"

"That's so sad!"

She smiled warmly. "Sometimes it is. But this story is more of a reminder that it can also help to put your own hurts and miseries in perspective, knowing that everyone has those feelings sometimes. But just look at the stars, girls: let them help you put things in perspective. I can't possibly feel lonely when looking at the stars."

As we read more and more of her books, and heard more and more of her own personal stories, we began to see how connected they were. Many of her own experiences were given to Camilla in *Camilla Dickinson*, Katherine in *A Small Rain*, and Flip in *And Both Were Young*. Many of her own characteristics were given to Meg in *A Wrinkle in Time* and Vicky in *Meet the Austins*.

This is the Chateau where we spent my twelfth summer, and I want to write a book about it someday. It's also the chateau of "The Small Rain," + "And Both were young," and above are the doors where Katherine went in to play the organ. I wish we had some photographs of the interior.

May 1, 1959

Reading Gran's early journals has brought her to us in a new and different way. Her voice, even as an eleven- and twelve-year-old, is recognizable, and watching her grow and struggle and change and commit through the pages has deepened our relationship with her. As both a teenager and an adult, she turned to her journal for multiple things: when she needed to just get something out of her head and onto paper, as a way of creating distance; when she needed a laboratory for investigating a character or narrative device; as a record of the books she was reading. From the time she was eighteen to the end of her life, she also used her journal as a way to reminisce and reimagine the past. She frequently reread her journals to cull information and incidents for her other writing, both fiction and nonfiction. Sometimes she edited her early journals with notes and thorough redactions, making certain passages impossible to read.

Her mother, Mado, kept most of the letters her daughter wrote to her, and in those days before email, when long-distance phone calls were expensive, Madeleine wrote almost every day, at least when she was in college and first on her own in New York. When she was a younger adolescent, her parents had had to threaten and cajole her for news from their only child. As a thirty-year old, Madeleine was still being encouraged and scolded by her mother.

Mado's visits to the Northeast were frequent, though. She finally moved into the guest room in Crosswicks in the summer of 1971 to spend her last few months on earth with her daughter and grandchildren. Madeleine's love for her mother is reflected in her memoir *The Summer of the Great-Grandmother*, published in 1974.

Madeleine was in her fifties in the 1970s when Hugh was cast as Dr. Charles Tyler in the daytime soap opera *All My Children*, and now when they traveled, he was recognized. Together they went to South America, China, Europe, and all over the United States.

When Hugh died in 1986, after forty years of marriage, Madeleine was devastated, but she responded in the way she always did when she was feeling something strongly: she wrote. She traveled even more after Hugh was gone, though New York was always home base, and we, her granddaughters, lived with her there until 1994. She still spent time at Crosswicks, where her son, Bion, lived. When Bion died in 1999, the same year she became a great-grandmother, she lost much of the wind in her sails, but continued to write and travel as long as she was able to. She died in 2007, just shy of her eighty-ninth birthday.

She always said that her stories knew more than she did, that she wrote to find out what she thought about things, that truth and fact were not the same. She also said she recognized that her books had lives of their own, far apart from her. She was deeply moved when another artist adapted her work, setting a poem to music, drawing a picture of a character, or taking one of her stories to stage or screen. She knew what a rarity and honor it is to have a book spark such a

Madeleine and Hugh, circa 1977

response in readers, and she felt it to be both a privilege and a responsibility.

Just as she never stopped growing and becoming *more* Madeleine, she challenged us and all of her readers to become more themselves, too, by finding the courage to be both creative and vulnerable. Children, she believed, were much better at this than grown-ups, and part of her true gift was not forgetting those parts of herself as she grew older. In *A Circle of Quiet* (1972) she reflects:

> I am still every age that I have been. Because I was once a child, I am always a child. Because I was once a searching adolescent, given to moods and ecstasies, these are still part of me, and always will be. Because I was once a rebellious student, there is and always will be in me the student crying out for reform.
>
> This does not mean that I ought to be trapped or enclosed in any of these ages, the perpetual student, the delayed adolescent, the childish adult, but that they are in me to be drawn on; to forget is a form of suicide; my past is part of what makes the present Madeleine and must not be denied or rejected or forgotten.

May all of us accept, embrace, and remember. And in Vicky Austin's words:

> *Each tree and leaf and star show how*
> *The universe is part of this one cry,*
> *That every life is noted and is cherished,*
> *And nothing loved is ever lost or perished.*

Léna and Charlotte
Photo by Amy Drucker

Authors' Note

Writing this book has been quite a journey. We were reluctant at first to try to tackle our grandmother's biography. After all, she herself spoke and wrote about her life a good deal, and we were aware of the fact that the lines between fiction, nonfiction, and memoir can be blurry, for our grandmother no less than for everyone else. How could we write about her in a way that would bring her to life in all her contradictory richness? That would do her justice and honor? That would be honest and fair?

There is something very special about the best grandparent-grandchild relationships. There can be friendship and love without the burdens of daily care and expectations that are so often present between parents and children. She delighted in us and loved us in such a way that we felt truly Named. This book was written out of love in return.

Part of loving someone is being able to see them clearly, and accepting them in all their imperfect fullness. Madeleine often said that she, like Meg Murry, could be both myopic and naïve about people. She never understood why some of her family bristled at *Ilsa*, or how the line walked between fact and fiction in *Meet the Austins* was hurtful to her children.

We decided to end the narrative with the publication of

A Wrinkle in Time for several reasons. It marked a new stage in her life and career; we thought younger readers would be most interested in her younger days, as we were when we were in school; and we wanted to respect the privacy of her journals and travel gently through them, especially those from the time when we knew her.

We did make one adjustment for the sake of narrative clarity: while we refer to Madeleine's mother as "Mado," that was because two Madeleines made the story confusing, and so we gave her the French nickname that her own grandmother was known by.

We hope that this book is recognized as an act of love on our part, and we want to thank the people who made it possible for us to see that this was something we could do: Léna's immediate family (husband Rob and children Cooper, Finn, and Scarlett); Charlotte's immediate family (husband John and children Kosta and Magda); our mother, Josephine; and brother, Edward. Additionally, Charlotte wishes to thank Barbara Braver and Catherine Hand for their support and encouragement. Léna is grateful for her Writopia family—both her colleagues and her students, who challenge her to be creative and vulnerable.

Many thanks to our agent, Lisa Erbach Vance; our editor, Margaret Ferguson; and the rest of the team at FSG, including Melissa Warten, Roberta Pressel, Janet Renard, Jennifer Sale, Mary Van Akin, Amanda Mustafic, Caitlin Sweeny, Melissa Zar, and Grace Kendall.